The Anatomy of Psychotherapy

SYSTEMS OF COMMUNICATION AND EXPECTATION

The Anatomy of Psychotherapy

SYSTEMS OF COMMUNICATION AND EXPECTATION

By HENRY L. LENNARD
and ARNOLD BERNSTEIN
with HELEN C. HENDIN, M.D.,
and ERDMAN B. PALMORE

COLUMBIA UNIVERSITY PRESS
New York, 1960

Published in Great Britain, India, and Pakistan
by the Oxford University Press
London, Bombay, and Karachi
Library of Congress Catalog Card Number: 60-7820
Manufactured in the United States of America

To

Elaine L. Lennard

and to

Alfred Kestenbaum, M.D.

Preface

Analysts and psychotherapists in general are keenly aware of the need for research in the processes of psychotherapy, and also of its difficulties. For, while everything they do is experimental in the sense that it is carefully considered, and the results of an intervention are carefully observed and pondered, in another sense, public access to these experiments, the discovery of subjective bias, the operational definition of variables, the quantification of results, as well as the teaching of the art, are all peculiarly difficult. Many therapists will take heart from this book. It breaks a new trail and shows the feasibility of a research approach that can be adapted by others and expanded indefinitely.

The authors report that when they set out with the hope of delineating some of the main features of the "anatomy of psychotherapy" they found that verbatim protocols of therapy sessions for extended series did not exist in sufficient number to make an analysis possible. In a way this was fortunate, since it forced them into a clear demonstration that by advance arrangements with patients and therapists tape recording could be acceptably integrated into the therapeutic process, on the one hand, and on the other, that the resulting miles of tape could actually be transcribed and analyzed by a research team —an unusual dual achievement, as those who try to deal technically with the fleeting stuff of human interaction will realize.

The feasibility or even desirability of tape recording under various conditions of therapy is an issue which is by no means resolved. It may be hoped that the results of these researchers will encourage others who have been wistful but so far restrained, to try sound recording in their own situation. There are justifiable reservations, not only as to the introduction of the tape recorder into therapy, but perhaps even more as to the transcription and analysis of verbatim protocols. More than one trunkful of sound recordings has been reluctantly consigned to the attic by researchers who found that they were simply not prepared to deal with the tireless output of a sound recorder. The fact is that without technical means of content analysis the researcher is in a somewhat worse position with recordings than as a witness to the first-hand situation, since he cannot see what is going on, and can not even hear as well.

But those with reservations about sound recordings and verbatim transcriptions will take encouragement and inspiration from the authors' successful adaptation and invention of methods of content and process analysis. A certain amount of courage is required to believe that by setting up categories that make only rather simple and obvious distinctions with regard to the single instance one may get something back by sorting and counting that will give him a new insight. The transition from a quantitative treatment of occurrences that seem simple and self-evident on the level of the single instance to a result that suddenly surpasses our previous understanding, is a subtle and fascinating one. The reader of this book can vicariously share in this experience.

To experience this transition in his own work is a reward for which every researcher might hope. But it is a reward premised on self denial. To obtain it, if at all, one must give up the pleasure of believing that he can understand everything at once from the grand vantage point of the eagle, and accept instead the plodding way of the burro. Those who do research in psychotherapy may find some useful procedures for content analysis already shaped to their needs in this study, and others they can adapt and further develop. The questionnaires for the measurement of role expectations of the patient and the therapist, and the relations of these expectations to the later interaction will give suggestions to sociologists and others concerned with the study of social roles in other settings.

Many sociologists will be gratified with the increase in operational substance of the concept of "system" as a result of this work. Both changes in behavioral process that occur much more quickly than the average tempo of social interaction, and those that occur much more slowly, tend to elude conscious awareness and control. The recognition of "unconscious" processes has thrown a good deal of light on the nature of behavioral processes in microscopic time spans. The recognition of "system properties" throws the searchlight in the direction of slower changes in longer time spans. With regard to these latter, in particular, perhaps, a quantitative approach may help to bring within cognitive grasp changes and relationships that otherwise escape attention. The sociologist is naturally eager to draw attention to these relationships. His "news to the world" is that system properties make a difference in the developing form of behavioral processes—just as the message of the dynamic psychologist is that unconscious processes make a difference. There is no necessary conflict between these two points of view. Should we not rather suppose that the increase of conscious control of behavioral processes will require an expansion of awareness of their developing form, both in more microscopic and more macroscopic time spans?

The conception of a scale of ever-increasing time spans within which the form of behavior develops, is maintained, and changes, will surely help to give substance to the aspirations toward integration which one finds so prevalent among behavioral scientists today. The present work helps to fill out, by concrete measures and examples, a portion of this time scale that is only dimly seen, and poorly related to more well known portions of the spectrum. It is not an accident, nor merely a hopeful gesture, that the authors of this study draw on ideas and methods from areas as diverse as psychoanalysis, clinical psychology, information theory, the study of interaction in small groups, the theory of feedback systems, learning theory, content analysis, role theory, theory of social systems, and general system theory. These areas begin to link up with each other naturally as one studies behavior as a process maintaining or changing its form in time. The authors have produced in their study, concrete and particular as it is, a tangible contribution to the integration of the sciences—and the arts—of human behavior.

ROBERT F. BALES

Cambridge, Massachusetts
November 28, 1959

Acknowledgments

We want to express our gratitude to the patients and therapists who cooperated in the study upon which this book is based. As will be apparent to the reader we have been greatly stimulated and influenced by the ideas and research of Gregory Bateson, Robert F. Bales, Ludwig von Bertalanffy, Robert K. Merton, Talcott Parsons, and John P. Spiegel, M.D.

This work has also been greatly aided by the cooperation of Harold A. Abramson, M.D., Merton Gill, M.D., Charles Y. Glock, George Hull, M.D., Lia Knoepfmacher, Clara Shapiro, and Hyman Spotnitz, M.D. We want to express special appreciation to Harold A. Abramson, M.D., for the many helpful suggestions he has contributed to the research from its inception.

We also want to thank the following friends and colleagues who have read and commented upon various chapters of the book: Renee Fox, William A. Glaser, Gene Hawes, and William Martin. In particular, we want to express our deep appreciation to Robert K. Merton for providing us with so many creative suggestions after a critical reading of the final manuscript.

The National Institute of Mental Health, U.S. Public Health Service, supported the research under grant M 1076 (C1–C3). Without this support, the type of research reported in this book would not have been possible.

Mr. Robert Tilley of the Columbia University Press has been a welcome "gadfly" in the production of this book.

Mr. Louis Lieberman rendered able service in the final days of our work.

To the following publishers, we gratefully acknowledge permission to quote from original sources:

Basic Books, Inc., for permission to quote from *Theory of Psychoanalytic Technique,* Karl Menninger (1958); and *Toward A Unified Theory of Human Behavior,* edited by Roy R. Grinker (1956).

The Free Press, for permission to quote from *Family, Socialization and Interaction Process,* edited by Talcott Parsons and Robert F. Bales (1955); and *The Patient and the Mental Hospital,* edited by M. Greenblatt, D. J. Levinson, and R. H. Williams (1957).

The Antioch Press, for permission to quote from *Life, Language, Law,* edited by Richard W. Taylor (1957).

Harvard University Press, for permission to quote from *Toward a General Theory of Action,* edited by Talcott Parsons and Edward A. Shils (1952).

W. W. Norton and Co., for permission to quote from *The Psychiatric Interview,* Harry Stack Sullivan (1954); and *Disturbed Communication,* Jurgen Ruesch (1957).

American Journal of Psychoanalysis, for permission to quote from "The Problem of Values in Psychoanalysis," John R. Reid, XV (No. 2, 1955).

Sociometry, for permission to use parts of the paper "Similarities of Therapist and Patient Verbal Behavior in Psychotherapy," Erdman Palmore, Henry L. Lennard, and Helen C. Hendin, XXII (No. 1, March, 1959).

Contents

Figures

Tables

In this connection it is not irrelevant to note that, of all forms of mental activity, the most difficult to induce . . . is the art of handling the same bundle of data as before, but placing them in a new system of relations with one another by giving them a different framework.

BUTTERFIELD, *The Origins of Modern Science*, p. 1

I would advise you to set aside your therapeutic ambitions and try to understand what is happening. When you have done that, therapeutics will take care of itself.

FREUD, letter to van Ophuijsen

It is not thy duty to complete the work, but neither art thou free to desist from it.

The Talmud, Ethics of the Fathers, II, 21

Introduction

For the past four years, a series of studies of communication between psychotherapists and their patients has been under way at Columbia University's Bureau of Applied Social Research.

The basic idea prompting the research was to apply concepts and methods developed within the framework of the social sciences—especially concepts pertaining to the study of face-to-face interaction and methods pertaining to the analysis of communication—to the study of psychotherapy.

Our position is that the social sciences and the depth psychological fields (such as psychiatry and clinical psychology) have developed concepts useful for description and analysis of human interactions of all kinds, whether they occur in a therapeutic setting, a work situation, an experimentally contrived problem-solving situation, a family setting, a political decision-making group, or a social work supervisory conference. In our view, many of the basic questions regarding the nature of interaction, communication, influence and change are the same for all the relationships listed.[1]

In the research described in the following pages, the direction of cross application of concepts and methods is from the social sciences to psychotherapy. We recognize that it would be equally productive to apply psychiatric concepts to social situations (e.g., work, play, family settings). This latter task, however, did not occupy us in our present work.

Our reasons for beginning the venture of cross-disciplinary application from the social sciences to psychotherapy are practical as well as theoretical. Social science concepts have not hitherto been applied to psychotherapy in any systematic fashion or with any major investment of effort. Moreover, psychotherapy represents a challenging and important social situation for study. Problems of emotional illness and its prevention and cure are currently of great concern to the society we live in. Psychotherapy is a special kind of social situation created specifically for the treatment and investigation of emotional illness.

Foremost among the theoretical considerations for the direction of our study is our conviction that social science concepts designed to describe phenomena of interaction and systems of relationships can make a major contribution to the understanding of therapy. We hope to gain greater perspective on the therapeutic relationship by going outside of the "postulates" or "theories" of the interacting partners. Social science concepts and methods can thus help to identify those factors in the therapeutic interaction which arise from the fact that therapy is a social situation, i.e., an interaction system.

Also of special significance for our work is the fact that in therapy verbal behavior is the major form of communication. Therefore, the methodological armamentarium available in the social sciences for the systematic, quantitative study of communication can be brought to bear upon the study of psychotherapy.

Still we did not focus on therapeutic problems of strategy, progress, and cure. For while the therapeutic practitioner has to make decisions with reference to therapeutic issues and cannot help but be engrossed in such questions, we were inclined to maintain a somewhat different attitude.

The study of how interaction and communication (verbal and nonverbal) between two individuals brings about change in one individual is still in its infancy. Many years of hard work still await the student of these processes before his concepts and tools can acquire precision. We believe that it is a mistake to try to focus on the most complex of these phenomena, growth and change (that is, the movement from ill health to well-being on the part of one participant through contact with another), without first being able simply to describe manifest overt occurrences between people.[2] To encompass the total interaction that takes place between a therapist and a patient is almost impossible. Since, however, there seems little doubt that language is the main instrument of therapeutic communication, we have concentrated our attention upon it.[3] An analysis of the role of visual cues, gestures, the physical situation, and other variables was not undertaken. Our research addressed itself specifically to a description in quantitative terms of the verbal interaction that takes place in the course of psychotherapy. This was done by recording eight therapies (four therapists with two patients each) for a period of eight months. More than 500 sessions were thus recorded. Over 120 of these sessions were subjected to an intensive analysis that resulted in the classification of more than 40,000 verbal propositions along several dimensions. Previous to and concurrent with therapy, each patient and therapist responded to eight questionnaires and interviews.

Without losing sight of the possibility of eventual application to practical issues, our major objective is represented by the title of this book, *The Anatomy of Psychotherapy; Systems of Communication and Expectation.*

This title suggests our emphasis—to provide a picture of the structure of therapeutic communication. Though process is considered in relation to change in structure, we are not primarily concerned with therapeutic results. In anatomy, structures can be identified by a student because the operational definitions and guides that are available make it possible for him to find them. In any delineation of structure, definitions must be precise enough so that students can identify and label the same physical attributes of the organism in the same way.

Much of the vocabulary of psychiatry has yet to achieve sufficient precision for students to accurately identify and label acts or sequences of acts occurring in psychotherapy on the basis of operational guides. Of course, students trained in the same tradition (e.g., adaptational school of analysis) may achieve such precision when concerned with one or another of the behaviors occurring in therapy (e.g., the identification of patient silence as resistance). But the basic anatomy or structure of psychotherapy remains undefined.

The design of categories precise enough for the identification by diverse observers of given types of therapist and patient behavior is one of the aims implied in our title, *The Anatomy of Psychotherapy.*

From the perspective of the social sciences, the focus in the study of therapy can be upon therapy as a system of action (verbal communication), upon therapy as a system of expectations, and upon the interrelations between communications and expectations. The informational aspects of the system of action (i.e., the input-output dimension which concerns the use of cognitive resources by the participants to carry out the goals of the interaction) are also given special attention in this book.

Therapy was thus approached in these four ways. Each focus gave rise to a series of questions which were dealt with in the research. Here are the specific perspectives assumed and the major questions asked:

I. Therapy as an ACTION SYSTEM

Does therapeutic interaction exhibit temporal differentiation, i.e., a uniform patterning of activities over time? Are there systematic longitudinal changes in the behavior of the therapist and patient pairs irrespective of the particular problem, personality, and therapeutic orientation of the participants?

In what respect is the type of differentiation occurring within the first eight months of therapy similar to or different from that occurring within an individual session?

How symmetrical, with respect to magnitude and kinds, are the verbal performances of therapist and patient? Who specializes in what kind of communication?

With respect to which communicational variables do interacting individuals become more alike in the course of psychotherapy?

What kinds of therapist communications reduce "strain" during therapy as a whole and thus keep the system from disintegrating?

Which therapist-patient variables exhibit a stable relationship within the session, i.e., maintain a fairly constant ratio?

How does disequilibrium or strain occurring within one session affect the structure of communication occurring within the subsequent session?

II. Therapy as an INFORMATIONAL EXCHANGE SYSTEM

How can therapist and patient communication be characterized in terms of information transmitted? What dimension of therapist and patient informational output can be studied systematically and objectively in the therapy situation?

What is the effect of therapist informational specificity upon volume of patient verbal output, patient verbalizations about affect, and patient consistency in verbal response?

How do variations in the level of patient verbal output affect the informational specificity (structure) of therapist response? Does the therapist's informational output consistently vary in response to patient's lengthy verbalizations, brief verbalizations, and silences?

What generalizations can be made about informational feedback processes in the therapeutic system?

III. Therapy as a SYSTEM OF ROLE EXPECTATIONS

What are the salient dimensions of therapist-patient role expectations?

How initially different or similar are given kinds of therapist and patient expectations?

How does the patient's learning of the "patient role" within the therapist-patient system affect the patient's ability to function within other role relationships (deutero-learning in therapy)?

IV. INTERRELATIONS BETWEEN COMMUNICATION AND EXPECTATIONS

To what extent are the role conceptions of the therapists reflected in their communication with the patients, i.e., how much congruence is there between expectations and behavior during therapy?

How are dissimilarities in given expectations of therapist and patient reflected in the content of what is discussed in therapy?

Through what communicative acts and mechanisms are disequilibria in the system of initial expectations coped with or resolved in the system of communications?

What are the communicative characteristics of sessions which fail to meet the patient's expectations (sessions with which the patient expresses dissatisfaction)?

The processes with which we are concerned lie largely outside the awareness of the participants. To adapt an illustration which Parsons has used in another connection: When we communicate by means of the English language, we are not aware during the act of communication of some of the grammar and syntax principles which we are employing. With respect to language usage, we may be able to identify and acknowledge the principles of grammar we have been using if our attention is called to these principles. However, with respect to social processes, we may have to be convinced that such principles govern our interaction, as no such spontaneous acknowledgement occurs. Even when data is presented, it may not convince us that the patterns pointed out do indeed occur.

Now, let us illustrate the point made with respect to psychotherapy. Let us conceive of therapeutic interaction as a sequence of activities including verbal statements and other behavior. Therapist communication follows upon patient communication and patient communication follows upon therapist communication. The attention of both therapist and patient is focused upon limited aspects of the communication sequence. The therapist may attempt to understand the message in terms of its implication for describing the patient's pathology and the patient may scrutinize the therapist's words to discover how to cope with his life problems. By virtue of this conscious concentration upon one or several aspects of each other's behavior, the possibility of viewing this behavior simultaneously from other perspectives becomes progressively more difficult if not impossible. Consider first that we are not only talking about a single act. What about the relation between acts, both within shorter and longer time spans? What about changes in the relationship of these acts through time? What about the long-range relationships between expectations held and communication conveyed or received?

It appears to us that most of what occurs (or what can be said to occur on the basis of viewing the interaction from many frames of reference) must, of necessity, lie outside the cognizance of the participants in the therapy group. It is questionable whether all the processes not honored by awareness on the part of the participants are as relevant to the therapeutic task as are those on which attention is focused. However, the extent of their relevance cannot be determined a priori. It is here that a scientific observer who has the opportunity to study the same body of data again and again, who may review the same communicative acts from as many points of view as his imagination will permit, and who may arrange and cross-tabulate his material in a variety of sequences and patterns, can make an important contribution.

The observer can determine in what ways temporally separate and apparently unrelated events fit together in a pattern. He is in a position,[4] not enjoyed by any of the participants, to identify the often subtle effects of earlier occurrences upon subsequent features of the therapeutic system. It is precisely to these tasks that the study reported in this book addresses itself. The identification of processes latent in the system on a variety of levels should of course have practical importance aside from its theoretical significance. We want to stress with Homans that in conceptual reorientation a result cannot be adjudged "useful or useless before it is used. Here, as at play, one must practice what Coleridge called 'the willing suspension of disbelief.'"[5]

We suspended judgment as to the potential usefulness of a viewpoint or concept until we had occasion to quantify the therapeutic data and to learn whether or not some new insights, either in the form of answers to old questions or in the form of new questions, resulted from the application of the concept.

We hope that this book will be of interest to the practicing therapist in psychiatry, psychology, and social work because of its focus on structure and process rather than on content and pathology. This book is also intended for sociologists and other social scientists concerned with the methodology and theory of interaction processes. It suggests measures for important but hitherto non-quantified dimensions of communication such as communication about social roles and informational characteristics. The student of the small group may also want to compare normative data from therapeutic interactions presented in this book with data from other problem-solving groups. Finally, researchers in the field of psychoanalysis, psychiatry, and communication processes should be stimulated, since many of the findings offer hypotheses for further research.

NOTES

1. The development of this approach has been immeasurably aided by the work of social scientists such as Leonard Cottrell, Freed Bales, Gregory Bateson, and Talcott Parsons; psychiatrists such as Harry Stack Sullivan and John Spiegel; and biologists such as Ludwig von Bertalanffy. Though our effort is on a much more modest scale than that of Bertalanffy's development of a general system theory applicable to physical, biological, and social systems, yet the direction of his work is very relevant to ours and helps to clarify our own position. The quotations which follow are from: Bertalanffy, "General System Theory," *Life, Language, Law*, ed. by Taylor.

> A first consequence of the existence of general system properties is the appearance of structural similarities or isomorphies in different fields. There are correspondences in the principles which govern the behavior of entities that are, intrinsically, widely different. . . . [p. 29]
>
> The isomorphy we have mentioned is a consequence of the fact that, in certain aspects, corresponding abstractions and conceptual models can be applied to different phenomena. It is only in view of these aspects that system laws will apply. This does not mean that physical systems, organisms and societies are all the same. In principle, it is the same situation as when the law of gravitation applies to Newton's apple, the planetary system, and the phenomenon of tide. This means that in view of some rather limited aspects a certain theoretical system, that of mechanics, holds true; it does not mean that there is a particular resemblance between apples, planets and oceans in a great number of other aspects. . . . [p. 61]

2. It seems to us now, in retrospect, that perhaps researchers in the field of psychotherapy and human relations have been overzealous in their pursuit of the more subtle facets and nuances of the

therapeutic relationship, without having first taken note of the more obvious and gross features. A simple and direct approach to the data seemed wisest before undertaking a more complex strategy.

3. Bernstein, "On The Nature of Psychotherapy," *Doubleday Papers in Psychology.*

4. Ibid.

5. Homans, *The Human Group,* p. 44.

Part One

THEORY AND METHODOLOGY

CHAPTER I

Conceptual Framework of the Study

Section 1. System Concepts

THE CONCEPT OF SYSTEM

In the pages that follow, eight two-person psychotherapy groups are examined as if each constituted a "system" within which many "sub-systems" could be identified. "System" has been variously defined as "any arbitrarily selected set of variables,"[1] as a "complex of elements standing in interaction,"[2] and more specifically as "two or more units related such that a change in the state of any one unit will be followed by a change in the state of the remaining units which in turn is followed by a change in the state of that unit."[3]

The notion of interdependence between variables rather than a unilateral relationship between variables is central to the concept of system. Interdependence, in the words of Parsons, "consists in the existence of determinate relationships among the parts or variables as contrasted with randomness of variability. In other words, interdependence is *order* in the relationship among the components which enter into a system."[4]

Implicit to a system is a span of time. By its very nature a system consists of an interaction, and this means that a sequential process of action and reaction has to take place before we are able to describe any state of the system or any change of state.

But before we could identify a particular system, we had to decide what was to be considered the unit and what was to be defined as the system. A decision as to what represents a unit is certainly an arbitrary one. One can think of units as "variables" in the sense that they can be measured at several given moments in time. The precision of measurement may of course differ, depending on the kinds of units involved. One can precisely and numerically measure a variable of verbal communication such as the number of words in a therapist statement. One can also measure a variable of expectation, such as how much activity the patient expects from the therapist in a given session, by asking if more, less, or about the same amount of activity is expected. Though the precision of measurement is higher for a variable in the system of communication than for a variable in the system of role expectations, both types of variables are particles in their respective systems, e.g., length of verbalization is a unit in the communicational system; amount of activeness expected is a unit in the expectational system.

Since that which is considered the unit of a system, and that which is considered the system, depend upon arbitrary definition, we approached the problem on two levels.

On the one hand, our units consisted of two individuals interacting in their respective roles as therapist and patient. The therapeutic system was conceived of as a dyad. This is the traditional way of conceiving of social systems as constituted by the reciprocal roles of its members. On the other hand, specific therapist and patient variables (e.g., communicative acts of given kinds, types of role expectations) were sometimes considered as the units and their interrelation as comprising a system. This is as legitimate as speaking on the one hand of the organism as a system, and then discussing the circulatory system, the respiratory system, and so forth. Once it is suspected that two or more variables vary in some determinate fashion, it would appear justified to view them as constituting a system and then to test whether such an approach adds to our understanding of the problem under investigation.

We suspect that there are at least as many variables involved in any single two-person interaction system as in the functioning of a single human organism. John Spiegel draws our attention to the large number of variables involved in even the simplest social system when he speaks of the "multi-level conversations"[5] occurring simultaneously between two persons interacting with each other.

At any given time one could focus on the semantic, formal, or content characteristics of a communication; on the overt vocal, gestural, and body tonus characteristics; or on the covert expectations and purposes accompanying its presentation.

With respect to the number of variables involved, the levels at which they can be examined and studied, the range and extent of interrelatedness, and the changes and movement in interrelationship, an enduring social relationship may indeed present problems of the same order of complexity as posed by the study of the human organism.

These remarks are not meant to imply that we were so ambitious as to try to cope with all of this complexity and to unravel it all, but only to draw attention to our own awareness that a global definition of a system and system components does not do justice to such enormous complexity.

THE CONCEPT OF EQUILIBRIUM

The order in the interrelationship among the units of the system possesses a "tendency to self-maintenance, which is very generally expressed in the concept of equilibrium. It need not, however, be a static self-maintenance or stable equilibrium. It may be an ordered process of change—a process following a determinate pattern rather than random variability relative to the starting point." [6,7]

Equilibrium is ". . . a state of a system such that there is a zero change of the units relative to each other." [8] The conception of equilibrium which we consider relevant to diagnosis and understanding of human interaction processes—whether within therapy or without—is the notion of *dynamic* equilibrium, which means the tendency of the system to maintain a steady state.[9] This version of the equilibrium concept appears closely related to Cannon's notion of "homeostasis" which describes the tendency of organismic systems to maintain their "essential variables within physiological limits." [10] Though blood sugar levels or body temperature levels continually fluctuate as a result of disturbances brought about by factors impinging upon these systems, concentration of glucose within the blood and the level of body temperature is maintained within given limits.[11] The sociological restatement of this conception of equilibrium in connection with systems of action (communication) would be that "there appears to be something underlying the observed overt behavior which has a continuity and persistence through time. It seems to act like an accounting system which takes account of deficits and surpluses that appear within given small time spans in such a way as to tend toward restoration of certain balances in quality and distribution of action among members over long time spans." [12]

Or put more simply, ". . . if two people relate to each other at all, they become involved in a system of transaction characterized by mutually regulative processes . . ." [13]

In the views advanced by Bertalanffy [14] and Nagel,[15] the human organism represents an "open system," not stabilized at a resting state, but subject to a continuous stream of internal and external stimuli and capable of "active behavior" (growth). Social systems may be similarly viewed as "open systems." We would like to advance the hypothesis that such "social organisms" (systems) are probably in some respects more "open" and capable of "growth" than individual organisms. Thus, when looking for equilibrium mechanisms in social systems, we do not expect to find the limits of "essential" variables to be as fixed and definite as, say, the limits of blood sugar concentration. For example, at a given age of a child, the ratio of parental activity to the child's activity might be maintained at a certain level. However, this ratio might be radically altered after a few years (when the child is treated more as an equal), but we would expect to observe at any given time a tendency to maintain the activity ratio within given limits.

We investigated equilibrium processes in at least three ways:

1. At the level of communicative acts, we searched for the equilibrium process in the interrelations of observable verbal behaviors of the therapist and patient during therapy.

2. At the level of role relations, we searched for equilibrium processes regulating and maintaining the therapist and patient role expectations. The data used were restricted to those gathered from periodic interviews with therapists and patients.

3. We also expected that equilibrium processes would mediate between the two levels. Disturbances in the expectational system (e.g., major discrepancies of given expectations of therapist and patient) may be repaired through exchange of verbal communication. By the same token, problems experienced in verbal communication would be reflected in the state of the system of expectations.

THE CONCEPT OF DIFFERENTIATION

The concept of differentiation has two major meanings. In the first sense, differentiation is defined as a temporal or phase phenomenon in which the behavior of the participants is seen to differ systematically over time (T_1, T_2, T_3, . . . T_n). In the second sense, differentiation is defined as specialization of behavior of participants at a given point in time, T_1 or T_2 or T_3. In the latter case, cross-sectional rather than longitudinal differentiation is observed.

Temporal Differentiation. We have already stated that the notion of system implies a temporal sequence, and thus change over time. Moreover, this change is not random, but exhibits a definite order. Interaction, for example, is described as a "sequence of qualitatively different activities of human individuals which is distributed in time and between individuals in such a way that seems to be organized and patterned in a great number of ways." [16]

The concept of temporal differentiation implies, as experience bears out, that the distribution of communicative acts of individuals encountering each other for the first time will differ from the distribution of their communicative acts occurring on their tenth encounter. Change in the frequency of occurrence of certain communicative acts viewed in relation to the duration of the interaction permits us to assume *different* patterns of differentiation for different systems (e.g., a problem-solving group, a friendship group, a therapy group). It also directs our attention to *uniformities* in the differentiation of communication exhibited among groups of the same type.[17]

With this concept, we were able to focus on the system properties of psychotherapy, instead of interpreting the vicissitudes of patient and therapist behavior in terms of psychological or ideological variables, as is traditional in psychiatric thinking.

The concept of differentiation is, of course, basic to the biological sciences. In embryology, differentiation is associated with *individuation* and *specialization* (e.g., cells of general potentiality develop into specialized cells as mass movement is replaced by individual movement). This differentiation includes not only temporal differentiation as defined above, but also specialization in structure. We would now like to suggest that a differentiation analogous to biological differentiation can be demonstrated in therapist-patient role conceptions and behaviors. It is evident to us that the asymmetry in therapist-patient role conceptions and behaviors is analogous to the *specialization* described in the biological sciences, while change in role conceptions and activities over time takes a form similar to biological *individuation.*

Differentiation as Specialization. Specialization then embraces the mode in which sociologists think of differentiation as the presence in social systems of patterns which are relatively constant through time. In a problem-solving group, for example, it is found that one member may be more specialized in the performance of leadership function than another who may specialize more in socio-emotional activity.

The concept of *symmetry* appears to be synonomous with the idea of lack of differentiation in behavior of participants. We use it to refer to similarity in the magnitude and kind of communication offered by each of the role partners.

Section 2. The Concept of Information

Among the more interesting developments in contemporary theory and research on psychotherapy is the growing emphasis upon the processes of communication and information in two-person interaction systems. Most of the goals for which a therapy group is formed are accomplished by means of communication. Words are the instrumental acts by which a large part of such communication is accomplished. But while the ends accomplished through the medium of communication can be studied in themselves, the means (the process of communication) can also be subjected to scrutiny and some of its structure and dynamics laid bare.

In the present study, the psychotherapy interaction is conceptualized as an informational exchange system. Questions are raised as to how the process of information flow can be studied systematically and objectively, what the dimensions of information are, and what relationships obtain among such dimensions. We hypothesized that the amount and quality of information put into the system by the therapist was systematically related to the amount and quality of the informational output of the patient and thus to the informational output of the system as a whole.

An important methodological problem lay in devising the means by which the variable "information" could be defined and managed operationally. We defined and quantified the information passing between therapist and patient in the following ways:

1. Information was defined as something that makes change possible, as a stimulus transmitted from one to the other of a two-person system and affecting subsequent communicational acts. Specifically, information as here defined reduces uncertainty and provides a basis for choosing from among a range of equi-probable possible verbal responses. The more choices a message eliminates, the more information it contains. This is analogous to the way the concept of information is employed in information theory.[18]

Communication can be said to have taken place when information has passed from a sender (such as the therapist) to a receiver (such as the patient), or vice versa. When a therapist, for example, tells a patient, "Tell me about your dream," he has transmitted a message to the patient. The message contains information to the extent that it limits the range of possible alternative responses from which the patient may choose his reply. In summary, as "information" is being used here, it is something that enables an individual to make a choice from his own repertory of preexisting responses. Thus the range of possibilities (and hence the informational content) of a therapist message would differ considerably from patient to patient. To measure informational value in terms of message specificity, it was necessary to invent a system of categories that scaled the degree to which the statement set limits upon the reply.

2. Information was also defined as output or verbal activity per se. We considered a single idea or proposition as one unit of information, and measured the amount of information in a message or statement by counting the number of propositions or ideas it contained. Thus we assumed that a long statement (one containing many propositions) contained more information than a short statement (containing only one or two propositions). Actually, this assumption does not correct for redundancy. Insofar as psychotherapy systems are concerned, however, a patient is conceded to be producing more information when he talks freely than when he is silent, or says only a little.

3. Information was defined as message content. Such qualities of information as grammatical form, mode, and substantive content were measured. In this sense, messages can be classified in terms of different categories and information can be thought of in terms of qualitative differences among messages. Particular messages were categorized as referring to feelings, to the treatment situation, or to the family system.

Questions were then raised as to what, in informational terms, differentiated one type of communicational system from another (e.g., a psychotherapy system from an educational system), how an optimal output was maintained for the system as a whole, and what the relation between given types of therapist and patient outputs must be in order to achieve a "satisfactory" level of total output. A major question studied was how much therapist informational output is necessary to maximize patient output and thus the efficiency of the system as a whole. Ruesch states that ". . . the foremost criterion of successful communication consists of the presence of feedback circuits which provide an opportunity to relay back to the original sender the effects that a statement has had upon other participants." [19]

Feedback involves some sort of informational *return* from one to the other partner in the communication system. Feedback in quantitative terms refers to the ratio of give to take, or in other words, to the level of informational reciprocity which must be established and maintained for a system to continue.

On the basis of this conceptual scheme, we undertook an examination of the effects of varying amounts of therapist feedback upon volume of patient output, and of the effect of increased and diminished patient verbal output upon the structure of therapist informational behavior.

Section 3. Role Expectations, Socialization, and Deutero-Learning

ROLE EXPECTATIONS

Sociologists maintain that, "The essence of any social situation lies in the mutual expectations of the participants. Every culture evolves . . . mores to cover typical situations, thus furnishing a pattern for the mutual expectations of the interacting parties." [20] Role expectations describe expectations held by a person in a given social status (e.g., therapist) vis-a-vis a person in another specified status (e.g., patient). Every individual occupies multiple statuses (such as patient, husband, artist), and according to Merton each one of these statuses involves "an array of roles." [21] For example, an individual occupying the status of teacher is involved in role relationships with students, other teachers, administrators, and so forth. Any particular role relationship implies a set of reciprocal expectations regarding the rights and obligations of the role partners (e.g., the physician expects to be paid for his services and the patient expects to pay).

From a sociologist's view, role expectations are defined by the social norms applying to the situation. The social norm sets forth that if one partner acts in a particular way, then such and such a response should follow from the other.

Role expectations in therapy are viewed in at least three senses:

1. Expectations in the normative sense (how the therapist should behave, determined by medical and psychiatric training of the therapist).

2. Expectations in the sense of anticipation (because of early experiences, a patient may anticipate rejection by the therapist).

3. Expectations in the sense of wishes (the patient may know that he should not expect the therapist to make decisions for him, but he wants—desires—him to do so just the same).

In many respects, expectations are "complementary." As Spiegel says:

> The principle of complementarity is of the greatest significance because it is chiefly responsible for that degree of harmony and stability which occurs in interpersonal relations. Because so many of the roles in which any of us are involved are triggered off by cultural cues in a completely complementary fashion, we tend not to be aware of them. We enact them automatically, and all goes well. This automatic function of role systems has significance for psychological economy of effort. We are spared the necessity of coming to decisions about most of the acts we perform because we know our parts so well.

But he goes on to say:

> However, it is a part of the human condition that high levels of equilibrium figured by precise complementarity of roles are seldom maintained for long. Sooner or later disharmony enters the picture. Complementarity fails; the role systems characterizing the interpersonal relations move toward disequilibrium.[22]

The psychotherapy situation is an example of a system of role relations in which initial complementarity is largely absent. This is due to a number of circumstances.

In the first place, the average person has little detailed information about the nature of psychotherapy. It is not as subject to public observation as are marital, friendship, or work relationships. Secondly, it is highly structured and complex, a relationship in which—it is claimed—one has to participate before one can completely grasp its requirements. Thirdly, the very problem which brings the patient to therapy—an inability to grasp adequately and to function appropriately within role relationships, together with rigidity of anticipation—makes it difficult for him to acquire a realistic set of initial expectations even though the opportunity to do so may have existed. Fourthly, something within the dynamics of the therapy process—its transference aspects—elicits expectations in the patient which cannot be met in the context of a professional relationship. And finally, normative expectations held by therapists are more clearly defined and structured than those of patients. Thus, there are likely to be basic discrepancies between the initial expectations held by therapists and patients.

Discrepancies in role expectations are thus a natural condition of therapeutic systems of role relations. Such discrepancies in expectations and the resultant system strain are hypothesized by us to reflect themselves in role *performances* (verbal behavior during therapy).

We did not attempt a complete identification of the great array of expectations held by therapists and patients. We limited ourselves to those expectations germane to the therapist and patient in their statuses of therapist and patient, and most particularly to expectations regarding the behavior required of the patient in order for him to function in the patient status within therapy.

SOCIALIZATION

In order for a therapeutic system to begin to function, it is first necessary for the patient to be inducted into the patient "role," that is, to acquire the set of role expectations which are reciprocal to those of the therapist.

The learning of a social role is referred to by sociologists as "socialization." Socialization, as defined by Merton, "designates the processes by which people selectively acquire the values and attitudes, the interests, skills and knowledge—in short, the culture—current in the groups of which they are, or seek to become, a member. . . . Socialization takes place primarily through social interaction with people who are significant for the individual." [23] In our view, a therapist's task as a socializer is analogous to that of a parent socializing a child into the family or of a teacher socializing a student to the school situation.

It is clear that socialization of the patient into the "patient role" is one of the crucial and necessary tasks in the construction and maintenance of therapeutic systems.

A set of questions follow from this view:

(1.) With respect to what kinds of expectations is the patient to be socialized? (2.) What is it about the therapy situation that makes role learning on the part of the patient possible? (3.) What "therapeutic goal" is made possible through such socialization?

(1.) One way of formulating the problem faced by the participants in therapy, and perhaps by all participants in role relationships, is in terms of learning who is to perform, to what extent, when, and with what kinds of performances. In terms of expectations this problem may be reduced to the following dimensions:

Activeness. How much of the job of verbalization is to be done by each?

Differentiation in Performance through Time. When does responsibility for communication shift from participant to participant?

Selectivity. What communications are appropriate and relevant? Since therapy differs from other situations, the patient must learn what types of subject matter are considered relevant and what kinds irrelevant.

Timing. We also gave thought to a more general dimension referring to expectations concerning the total duration of the therapeutic relationship and the time required to accomplish specific therapeutic goals.

(2.) Therapy favors clarification of expectations because its basic character is that of verbal interchange. Words are considered more economical than deeds in the clarification of mutual expectations in interpersonal relations, and therapists insist that patients put their thoughts and feelings into words. Thus, strain and dissymmetry of expectations are exposed. Communications containing information about the treatment situation are introduced to reduce the disparity between expectations. We are aware of Parsons' position that therapist manipulation of sanctions is important for patient socialization.

(3.) Dissymmetry of expectations not only interferes with the therapeutic task, but can actually lead to the premature death of a therapeutic system. Our data show that when overt discrepancies were too great with regard to timing expectations, treatment was terminated. For example, in two therapist-patient pairs that discontinued after a few sessions, the patients expected to be cured in a few sessions and the therapists expected a long treatment process.

One of the problems frequently mentioned in keeping uneducated patients from lower socio-economic strata in therapy is their inability to learn that in therapy, which is unlike other doctor-patient contacts, *they* must assume responsibility. An idea which presents great difficulty for them is that verbalization can represent the vehicle and goal of therapy.

From this point of view, learning the patient role—the rules of the game (the appropriate expectations and behavior)—precedes and continues concurrent with the substantive task of therapy, the "cure" of the patient. Though we have data to show that socialization is never fully achieved and continues through the later sessions of therapy, preoccupation with primary role definition and discussion decreases considerably over time. This can be taken to mean that some degree of expectational complementarity has been achieved and that attention is turned to the business of therapy. Now, this business of therapy —according to most analytic formulations—is also primarily concerned with therapist-patient relationships, but from a different angle. Discussion revolving around the patient's expectations of the therapist as a substitute (transference) object for persons significant in the patient's past, and the working through of "irrational fears and rigid defenses," occupy a central place in therapy, according to the analytic paradigm. To identify and examine such "transference" expectations and performances in great detail was beyond the scope of our book.

DEUTERO-LEARNING

Another view as to how the process of socializing a patient is related to the goal of therapy can be offered. It is based on Bateson's concept of "deutero-learning." This concept, which has also been described as "learning how to learn," refers to the fact that in any given learning situation, one learns not only what one is supposed to learn, but also something about the process of learning itself.

As Bateson puts this ingenious idea:

> It is a commonplace that the experimental subject—whether animal or man, becomes a better subject after repeated experiments. He not only learns to salivate at the appropriate moments, or to recite the appropriate nonsense syllables; he also, in some way, *learns to learn.* He not only solves the problems set him by the experimenter, where each solving is a piece of simple learning; but, more than this, he becomes more and more skilled in the solving of problems . . . we might say that the subject is learning to orient himself to certain types of contexts, or is acquiring "insight" into the contexts and sequences of one type rather than

another, a habit of "punctuating" the stream of events to give repetitions of a certain type of meaningful sequence.[24]

Examples of this phenomenon are abundant in fields as diverse as anthropology and classical learning theory (transfer of training).

Perhaps two brief illustrations will suffice here. In learning a foreign language, one not only learns the particular language but also about the process of learning a language. Each successive language is more easily mastered. Learning one card game prepares one for the learning of the next because one has not only learned the rules of the particular game, but also that card games involve—among other things—the distribution of cards among players, symbolic meaning of action, patterns of plays, different values of cards, the use of strategy and deception, and so forth.

In our view, deutero-learning occurs in the psychotherapy situation both in a general and in a specific manner. A patient's generic problem can be conceived of (among other things) as an inability to function adequately within major social role systems (family, occupational, and other systems). In other words, the patient is not properly socialized into his diverse roles, and has not acquired sets of expectations and behaviors that would permit social interaction to proceed smoothly.

In therapy, the patient not only "learns" a set of expectations appropriate to the therapeutic relationship and how to behave in accordance with such expectations, but in learning this—according to the deutero-learning concept—he acquires insight into the principles underlying the learning of role expectations in general. These principles are then available for use in learning or relearning other patterns of expectations governing relationships in which he participates. The therapeutic relationship seems to be peculiarly adapted to the task of deutero-learning.

Three major factors seem responsible for this: Firstly, there is the basic requirement that the patient in therapy verbalize all thought and feeling. Strain, frustration, and disappointment must be discussed and resolved. Secondly, the therapeutic relationship is unique in that it requires an entire socialization sequence to occur within a limited time span. Principles and rules can thus emerge with great clarity. Thirdly—and perhaps most important of all—the therapist is a skilled socializer. Unlike a parent who socializes one or two children, the therapist teaches the same role over and over again (i.e., the patient role). Through his training and his experience in many therapeutic role systems, he has a more clearly structured conception of the pattern of expectations required for functioning within therapy than have many other individuals who are charged by society with the task of role induction. He is thereby in a position to convey a clearer picture of certain social roles than most others. And of course, spatial and temporal insulation of the therapeutic situation minimize the amount of direct interference with and obstruction encountered by the therapist during his socializing efforts.[25] Other socializers are not nearly so fortunate.

We suggest that the four major dimensions involved in patient socialization into therapy (activeness, differentiation, selectivity, and timing) are to a considerable extent involved in all major role relationships. Role relationships require allocation of responsibility for activity and action among participants (activeness). Role relationships involve variations in behavior depending upon the length of time the relationship has persisted (differentiation). Role relationships involve decisions as to what subject matters and types of interaction may properly occur within them (selectivity). And lastly, role relationships involve estimates of the duration of therapy and the time needed for the accomplishment of goals (timing). We believe that in learning the patient role with respect to these four dimensions, the patient's learning with respect to these dimensions in other role relationships is facilitated. For example, having learned in therapy that he must accept responsibility for activity and participation, he is now sensitized to expectations with respect to activity and participation in other relationships. As a husband, for example, he may then be able to respond to his wife's expectations with regard to activity and participation and thus to assume his responsibilities in his marital role.

The concept of deutero-learning leads to a view of role learning in therapy not only as a precondition of therapeutic accomplishment but perhaps also as a major feature of therapy in the sense of "cure."

NOTES

Full references are given in the bibliography at the back of the book.

1. Ashby, *Design for a Brain,* p. 15.
2. Bertalanffy, "General System Theory," *Life, Language, Law,* ed. by Taylor, p. 60.
3. Zelditch, "A Note on the Analysis of Equilibrium Systems," *Family: Socialization and Interaction Process,* ed. by Parsons and Bales, p. 402.
4. Parsons and Shils, editors, *Toward a General Theory of Action,* p. 107.
5. Spiegel, "Interpersonal Influences within the Family," *Group Processes, Transactions of the Third Conference,* ed. by Schaffner.

> Most interpersonal events consist of multi-level conversations. Usually there is not just one conversation or one interaction going on. Nor is it simply a question of static levels, but rather of complex interweavings which have structure . . .

6. Parsons and Shils, editors, *Toward a General Theory of Action,* p. 107.
7. It is, of course, well known that the concepts of system, equilibrium, and the quite similar notion of homeostasis and adaptation were first developed and used in the biological and physical sciences (e.g., Claude Bernard, Walter B. Cannon, and others). They were then introduced into the social sciences, especially into anthro-

pology and sociology, and are now applied by social scientists to a consideration of psychotherapy. Some psychiatrists, notably Grinker, Ruesch, and Spiegel, have conceived of human interaction, in therapy and without, in these terms. It would appear that their interest in these concepts, although originating in their basic medical training, may have been intensified through interchanges with social scientists. Conferences such as the ones held under the auspices of the Josiah Macy, Jr., Foundation, which have been much attended by many of the above, have great significance for the cross-fertilization of the medical and social sciences. The above-mentioned psychiatrists also had an early interest in the so-called psychosomatic disorders, for which concepts of interdependence, equilibrium, and homeostasis seem especially relevant.

8. Zelditch, "A Note on the Analysis of Equilibrium Systems, *Family: Socialization and Interaction Process*, ed. by Parsons and Bales, p. 402.

9. Bertalanffy, "General System Theory," in *Life, Language, Law*, ed. by Taylor, p. 63.

> Every living organism is essentially an open system. It maintains itself in a continuous inflow and outflow, building up and breaking down of components, never being, so long as it is alive, in a state of chemical and thermodynamic equilibrium but maintained in a so-called steady state which is distant from the latter. . . . Obviously, the conventional formulations of physics are in principle inapplicable to the living organism *qua* open system and steady state . . .

10. Ashby, *Design for a Brain*, p. 57.

11. For a remarkable comment on the concept of homeostasis, we refer the reader to Emerson's statement: ("Homeostasis and Comparison of Systems," *Toward a Unified Theory of Human Behavior*, ed. by Grinker, p. 155):

> . . . The concept of homeostasis is complex. The physiological homeostasis within the body may apply to temperature; it may apply to sodium ions; it may apply to calcium ions; it may be applied to glycogen in the nerve; it may apply to sugar in the blood; it may be involved in neurophysiological mechanisms or biochemical mechanisms. It may include a hormone; it may incorporate gene systems; it may control nerve impulses. So it is a very complex concept to subsume under the one notion of self-regulation. Many different things are being regulated, not a few simple things. Some of these we know about physiologically, but unquestionably, innumerable aspects of physiological homeostasis are unknown still. One might almost say that it is such a big generalization that it does not have

direct utility as a concept. But I think quite the opposite. It is a remarkable concept in that you can objectively measure it and compare it. . . .

12. Bales and Slater, "Role Differentiation in Small Groups," *Family: Socialization and Interaction Process,* ed. by Parsons and Bales, p. 273.

13. Spiegel, "The Social Roles of Doctor and Patient in Psychoanalysis and Psychotherapy," *Psychiatry,* XVII (1954), 369–376.

14. Bertalanffy, "Some Biological Considerations on the Problem of Mental Illness," *Bulletin of the Menninger Clinic,* Vol. XXXIII, No. 2 (March, 1959).

15. Nagel, "A Formalization of Functionalism," *Logic Without Metaphysics.*

16. Bales, *The Strategy of Small Group Research,* mimeographed, undated.

17. Bales and Strodtbeck, "Phases in Group Problem Solving," *Journal of Abnormal and Social Psychology.*

18. Miller, "Psycholinguistics," *Handbook of Social Psychology,* ed. by Lindzey.

19. Ruesch, *Disturbed Communication,* p. 34.

20. Davis, *Human Society,* p. 83.

21. Merton, "The Role Set: Problems in Sociological Theory," *The British Journal of Sociology,* Vol. VIII, No. 2 (June, 1957), pp. 106–120.

22. Spiegel, "The Resolution of Role Conflict within the Family," *The Patient and the Mental Hospital,* ed. by Greenblatt, Levinson, and Williams, p. 548.

23. Merton, Reader, and Kendall, editors, *The Student Physician,* p. 287. See also Parsons, *The Social System,* p. 208.

24. Bateson, "Social Planning and the Concept of 'Deutero-Learning,'" *Science, Philosophy, and Religion, Second Symposium,* 1942.

25. Of course, even the psychotherapy situation is beset by outside disturbing influences, and its insulation is not so complete as might be wished. Interference from the patient's family is not infrequent and financial difficulties often intrude upon the smooth course of treatment.

CHAPTER II

Methodology

BIOGRAPHY AND DESCRIPTION OF THE RESEARCH

In the course of research during 1953, one of the authors (HLL) undertook to apply social science concepts and small group theory to actual psychotherapy data. To this end he required verbatim records of psychotherapy hours. During his search for materials for such an analysis, he located a few books containing case histories written by practicing therapists that seemed to be based upon some sort of verbatim data. However, investigation showed that most of the material actually represented reconstructions from notes taken during treatment. A few brief published cases by such authors as Rogers,[1] Wolberg,[2] and Deutsch [3] were indeed located and studied. Difficulties with most available published materials were that they had been slightly edited for publication and that uniform procedures for transcription had not been used. This made quantitative treatment of the verbatim data difficult. Several research and training centers in psychotherapy were then contacted in an attempt to locate verbatim records. It evolved that though many single hours of psychotherapy had been recorded and transcribed, sufficiently complete cases or continuous series of transcribed hours were not available. When case material was available, transcription techniques were not uniform or only a single case was recorded for a given therapist. Usually, collateral data had not been gathered concurrently with treatment from either the therapist or the patient regarding their subjective reactions to the treatment experience. There was in fact no body of psychotherapy data upon which to perform the proposed dissection. The problems inherent in an analysis of communication during psychotherapy are massive and complex. Before a quantitative and systematic attack on these problems could be undertaken, it was first necessary to collect the kind of data which would make such an effort possible. We thus found ourselves faced with the task of assembling a reasonably large body of verbatim psychotherapy data that would constitute a library of facts from which we could draw material to test our hypotheses.

It is of course not surprising that a body of such material did not already exist when the present research was initiated. Many practical, technical, and economic difficulties stand in the way of a researcher or group who seek an opportunity to collect a large mass of data. Without the support of the National Institute of Mental Health of the United States Public Health Service, our own study might not have materialized.

The number of cases that could be recorded and transcribed for the purpose of our study was limited by considerations of time and money. Ultimately, however, it became possible to obtain verbatim recordings of eight therapies over a period of almost a year each. While a sample of eight does not seem large, such a sample consists of well over 500 hours of treatment and contains tens of thousands of scorable communication units. Moreover, considering the dearth of existing samples of verbatim material on psychotherapy, the material recorded in eight continuous long-term therapies constitutes a massive amount of data.

THE PROBLEM OF GENERALIZATION FROM THE FINDINGS

It would probably be fair to say that we were not engaged primarily in a "fact finding" research but rather in a research designed to develop and test a methodology and to uncover hypotheses. Most of the findings that we report are not sample statistics to be generalized but parameters of our own group of eight therapist-patient pairs. When, for example, we report that a given variable decreases over time, we are not generalizing, but describing what actually happened to that variable within the group of cases we studied. Our primary concern was to see how far hypotheses about small groups, interaction systems, and other social science concepts could be fruitfully applied to psychotherapy groups. We derive some comfort from the fact that eight therapist-patient pairs is the largest number yet studied so extensively, but we do not suggest that they constitute a "sample" of psychoanalytic dyads, let alone that they are randomly drawn from the universe of psychotherapy groups in general.

The study, however, is multidimensional and multilevel, and the confidence that one can place in a generalization from the findings will vary with the dimension or level. Moreover, the number of cases also varies from level to level and category to category. In setting confidence limits, it should be borne in mind that different total numbers are involved in the "sample." There were only four *therapists* but there were eight *dyads*, 500 *sessions*, 5,985 *exchanges*, and 41,513 verbal *propositions*, coded along multiple dimensions.

The study of each therapist-patient pair can also be regarded as one case study. Thus, in a sense, each case study was replicated eight times. For some types of analyses, published transcripts were used for validation.

THERAPISTS

Four psychotherapists agreed to cooperate with the project for the purpose of data collection. Three of the four therapists have been or are currently affiliated with a psychoanalytic institute recognized by the American Psychoanalytic Association. The fourth therapist is a graduate of a program in Clinical Psychology approved by the American Psychological Association and has been in practice for more than ten years. No effort was made to select therapists in terms of a particular orientation. Though the cooperating therapists consider themselves to be working within a psychoanalytic framework, they differ considerably in relation to specific therapeutic issues.[4] Each therapist agreed to carry two patients for the project and to tape record continuously for the duration of the treatment, or one year, whichever was shorter. The therapists were free to accept or reject patients on the same basis as they would in their own practice.

PATIENTS

The patients in our project were referred from psychotherapy clinics in the New York City area. All were informed of the research nature of the project and agreed in advance of their first contact with the therapist to permit the recording of their hours and to fill out questionnaires from time to time. Their motivation in accepting these conditions was the promise of reduced fees and immediate treatment. They were assured that their anonymity would be preserved and that the material would be used only for the advancement of science and toward the improvement of psychotherapeutic practice. Since referrals and initial appointments were made by an intake supervisor, it was possible to record verbal interactions between the patient and his therapist from their very first contact. No patient referred to the project objected to these conditions and only once among all the hours did a patient request that an hour not be recorded. In the main, patients seemed to accept the fact of recording and did not express continuing consciousness or interest in it during the course of their treatment. Of the eleven patients accepted for the project, three discontinued treatment within the first eight sessions.

DATA

After the session was tape-recorded, it was transcribed verbatim, the typescript noting any and all sounds made by either of the participants, including all silences timed to the second, giggles, laughs, sighs, sobs, stuttering, and coughs. Any marked change in the voices was noted by underlining. If a word was unintelligible, an "x" was substituted in its place. Each verbal statement made by either a therapist or a patient was then classified, coded, and punched onto an IBM card. Pages in our typed manuscripts were prepared uniformly and thus could be used as a rough standard approximation of the number of words produced or the volume of a session.

In addition to the verbatim recordings of the therapy sessions, patients and therapists were interviewed prior to therapy and were given questionnaires to fill out at intervals during treatment. The interviews and the questionnaires sought information on role expectations of therapists and patients; how therapists and patients perceived and evaluated the interaction that had occurred during particular hours (thus similarities and dissimilarities could be compared), and how therapists and patients viewed their interaction in retrospect. In addition, therapists and patients executed an "inventory of values." The following sections constitute a summary of all our data sources other than the verbatim recordings:

1. (a) *Therapist Pre-Interview.* This interview was conducted with each therapist prior to his first contact with any of the patients. Questions were asked about the therapist's

role expectations both in the sense of how he ought to behave in psychotherapy and how he usually does behave in therapy. Specifically, we investigated therapist expectations as to:

amounts and kinds of activity considered appropriate to the therapeutic task;

types of relevant subject matter to be discussed;

how he would vary his behavior in relation to different phases of the therapy process, different patients, and different situational problems (e.g., depressed versus agitated patient);

how he would handle patient demands for affective reciprocity;

how he maintained the professional character of the therapeutic relationship.

(b) *Patient First Questionnaire.* This questionnaire was administered to the patient at the beginning of therapy.[5] Its main purpose was to ascertain the patient's expectations regarding the nature of psychotherapy; the patient's objectives in seeking psychotherapy; subject matter considered relevant to psychotherapy; types of activities in which the patient expected the therapist to engage; and the patient's knowledge regarding psychotherapy. This questionnaire allowed us to compare the patient's expectations with those of the therapist and to examine the effects of this similarity or dissimilarity on the subsequent interaction and change in conceptions.

2. *Therapist First Questionnaire.* This questionnaire was administered to the therapist after the second session with the patient. It asks the therapist to apply his general conceptions of therapy to the specific patient and to discuss what topics he expected would be most relevant; what behavior he would consider appropriate for the particular patient; in what areas the patient most needed help; how soon progress would be achieved; and so forth.

3. *Patient and Therapist Second (Value) Questionnaires.*

The value questionnaire was administered to the patient and therapist after their third session, and again to the patient during his third and fifth months of therapy. It asks the patient and therapist to check whether each of twenty listed objectives are very important, somewhat important, or not at all important; to check whether he agrees strongly, agrees, disagrees, or disagrees strongly with ten different value statements; and to list three characteristics each for a man and a woman whom they liked and admired. These questionnaires allowed us to compare the therapist and patient values. The earlier patient value questionnaire could be compared with his later questionnaire to study changes in values which might have occurred during his therapy.

4. *Patient and Therapist Third (Panel) Questionnaires.* These questionnaires were administered to the patient and therapist in the second, third, fourth, and fifth month of the therapy. The questionnaires were administered immediately after the close of the regular therapy session, and required the therapists and patients to describe and evaluate the previous hour in terms of who and what was talked about; what activities the therapist engaged in; the relevance of material discussed; satisfaction with communication; and the progress made. The questionnaires permit comparison for similarity and dissimilarity of therapist and patient evaluations. These questionnaires can be used to relate evaluation of an hour to the actual communicational structure of that hour. It is therefore possible to identify the patterning of communication in those hours which did not meet the patient's expectations.

5. *Patient and Therapist Fourth Questionnaires.* This questionnaire was administered to the patient and therapist during the sixth month of therapy, immediately after a regular therapy session. In addition to repeating most of the questions in the Third Questionnaire dealing with the immediately preceding session, this questionnaire asked the patient to describe the

previous five months of therapy in terms of whether the therapist had acted differently from what the patient expected; whether or not what the patient had expected to discuss was discussed; what the patient's current objectives in therapy were; and what areas the patient most wished clarified. Similar questions were asked of the therapist.

6. *Patient and Therapist Fifth (Final) Questionnaires.* This questionnaire was administered to the patient and therapist at the end of eight months. It asked patient and therapist to discuss the ways in which the patient had changed as a result of therapy and how much progress they believed the patient had made.

UNITS OF QUANTITY

Our task was to find methods for recording and analyzing the operations between the patient and the therapist and to find out which of these units of behavior were amenable to significant management. We could not reasonably expect any single method of examination to give us more than a limited amount of information and so we were willing to use as many methods as were required for the assignment.[6]

(1) *Proposition.* A proposition for the purpose of this study was defined as a verbalization containing a subject and a predicate either expressed or implied. It is the verbal expression of a single idea. Essentially the same definitions and instructions used by Bales,[7] Dollard,[8] Murray,[9] and others were used by our coders to separate the transcripts into propositional units:

(a) A proposition typically consists of an independent clause.

(b) "Uh-huh," "yes," "yeah," "mm-hm," etc., are counted as single propositions.

(c) Compound sentences joined by "and," "but," etc., are broken down into their component simple parts, each of which is scored as a proposition.

(d) If a single subject is followed by a series of predicates, a separate score is given for each predicate—the assumption being that each constitutes a new item of information. For example, the following sentence would be analyzed into four propositions: "This problem which we talked about in yesterday's session / impresses me as being very complicated / difficult / and perhaps beyond my power to solve."

(e) False starts do not count as separate units. The following sentence contains a single proposition: "I went, I went downtown yesterday."

In order to determine the reliability of unitization, the same therapy session was coded independently by two different coders. A total of 332 propositions was scored for the session by Coder *A* and 334 propositions for the session by Coder *B*, a difference of less than one percent.

(2) *Statement.* A statement is an uninterrupted sequence of propositions from either the therapist or patient. While therapist statements rarely consist of more than three propositions, patient statements sometimes contain more than 100 propositions. An example of how a patient statement was divided into propositions follows: "I spoke to Frank about the course work. / I told him I was interested in it. / It was stimulating to me. / I still do not know what the teacher is getting at."

The *quantity* of information contained in a statement is estimated by counting the number of propositions it contains. Previous research [10] has shown that number of propositions is correlated ($r = .8$) with such other units as number of words spoken, number of lines of typescript, etc.

(3) *Interaction or exchange.* An exchange or interaction is defined as a therapist statement followed by a patient statement, or vice versa. It may consist of several propositions but it represents a complete interaction. The number of exchanges per hour or per transcribed page is the *rate of interaction* and

provides a measure of the frequency with which a therapist speaks or interacts.

Each exchange was coded and punched onto a single IBM card. Since an exchange contains both a patient's statement and a therapist's statement, half of each IBM card was devoted to coded information about the therapist statement and half to coded information about the patient statement. This facilitated machine comparison of the kinds of patient statements that resulted from varying amounts and kinds of therapist statements, and conversely, the kinds of therapist statements that followed upon various kinds of patient statements.

INFORMATIONAL SPECIFICITY DURING PSYCHOTHERAPY

In approaching the problem of describing and quantifying the structure of the therapist's informational behavior, we have been guided by such formulations as the following by George Miller:

> The basic notion underlying the measurement of information is that information is something to reduce uncertainty. For example, imagine facing a choice among a large number of possibilities. Anything that gives information about the choice will reduce the number of possibilities. A message that reduces the number of possibilities a great deal gives a large amount of information.[11]

Any idea (proposition) expressed by a therapist may be regarded as a message sent to the patient by the therapist. Such propositions differ in the degree to which the information they supply provides a basis for limiting the range or array of possible responses. For example, the therapist statement, "Just start by saying anything that occurs to you," has a low specific informational stimulus value because it does not limit the patient's response to any specific subject matter or proposition. It may therefore be said to be nondirective or unstructured. On the other hand, the question, "How old are your sisters?," has a high specific informational stimulus value because it provides information that can be used to set limits on the range of possible alternatives from which the patient may select his reply. It therefore may be said to be highly directive or structured.

DESCRIPTION OF THERAPIST INFORMATIONAL BEHAVIOR

To adapt these notions to the study of the informational structure of the therapist's verbal output during psychotherapy, a set of eight categories was devised to roughly quantify the amount of structure or information contained in each therapist message. The amount of information contained in any therapist proposition is defined as its "informational stimulus value;" this corresponds to the extent to which it tends to place limits upon the array of verbal responses from which the patient may choose a reply. The categories are presented below in approximate order of their "informational value."

In addition to the definitions of the categories, illustrations are provided to demonstrate the kinds of therapist statements which would be classified into the particular category. In this way, the reader will be able to decide for himself whether he agrees with the stimulus value assigned to each category.

To get an estimate of coder reliability, a test was made by having two coders independently code a session chosen at random. They agreed as to category in 171 out of 208 decisions. In other words, they independently placed a therapist statement into the same category in 82 percent of the cases.

A description of categories relating to therapist informational specificity follows.

CATEGORY (1)

Definition: The therapist indicates that he is listening and *passively* encourages the patient to continue.

Description: "Yeah, I see," "Mm-hm," etc., are classified into this category. "Mm-hm" is used in the sense of encouraging the patient to talk further without limiting him in any way. The therapist does not provide any information that the patient can use to limit his choice of topics.

Illustration:

Patient: If there's much more of this emotional strain and stress, and I think that possibly there might be, then it's going to be very difficult by the end of the year.[12]

Therapist: Mm-hm. Category (1)

Patient: If I can just hang on and I have so far (pause), I have gotten so much out of the therapy, particularly the last couple of times—that I am very grateful that you were nondirective.

Therapist: Mm-hm. Category (1)

Patient: Because if you'd told me some of this stuff naturally I'd—I can build up my defenses so fast.

CATEGORY (2)

Definition: The therapist indicates that he is listening and *actively* encourages the patient to continue.

Description: Propositions such as, "You needn't be afraid to talk," and "Just start by saying anything that occurs to you," are classified into this category. The objective in the use of such propositions is to have the patient verbalize irrespective of subject matter. This category is the same as (1), except that the therapist is more active.

Illustration:

Patient: Where shall we begin?

Therapist: Wherever you feel like. Category (2)

Patient: Is there anything in particular that you'd like me to talk about?

Therapist: No, I just want you to talk about anything. Category (2)

CATEGORY (3)

Definition: The therapist limits the patient to a single subject matter area.

Description: Patient is limited to one subject matter area but within that area he can select from the range of information available to him. Propositions beginning with "why," "how," and "what" are usually classified into this category. This category places emphasis upon the limitation of the patient to a subject matter *area.*

Illustration:

Patient: My mind is a bit empty as regards myself. . . .
Therapist: How about talking about your work? Category (3)

Therapist: Have you had any thought about therapy? What did you think about last session? Category (3)

CATEGORY (4)

Definition: The therapist refers to a specific proposition which has already been introduced in either of the two immediately antecedent interactions.

Description: This category differs from category (3) because it limits the patient to a specific *idea.*

Illustration:

Patient: Well, in a way it seems there is nothing I can do about it.
Therapist: Ah, so you don't think you can do something about it. Category (4)

Patient: Well, I wouldn't do it until I could trust her.
Therapist: What does—what do you mean by trust her? Category (4)

Patient: It seems a funny thing to say, it got me wrong.
Therapist: Wrong in what sense? Category (4)

CATEGORY (5)

Definition: The therapist introduces a *new* proposition. This category differs from category (4) because the therapist takes the initiative in introducing a new idea.

Description: Though therapist propositions falling into this category are often structured so as to be logically satisfied by a "yes" or "no" answer or a single item of information, they are not actually intended to do this. For example, the proposition, "you sound depressed," is not ordinarily intended to solicit a patient reply such as, "yes, I am," or, "no, I am not depressed," but rather to stimulate the patient to react to the hypothesis formulated by the therapist.

Illustration:

Patient: What did she get married for?
Therapist: Maybe you disappointed her, you didn't ask her.
Category (5)

Therapist: You seem a little blue. Category (5)
Patient: Blue?
Therapist: Yeah. Category (1)
Patient: Not especially.
Therapist: I just thought you seemed somewhat down in the mouth.
Category (4)

Category (4) and Category (5) are somewhat similar in emphasis. Both rate the therapist's tendency to limit subsequent patient communication to specific propositions or items of information, without structuring the patient's response [as in Category (7)]. The reason for developing two categories for verbal stimuli of this kind lies in the fact that the subject of the therapist's propositions may be "old" or "new." It is considered "old" if it has already been introduced by the patient or the therapist in the same or similar form in one of the two antecedent exchanges. It is considered "new" if it does not appear in either of the previous two exchanges. The former type of therapist intervention is classified as (4) and the latter as (5), since it appears to us that having the patient come to grips with a hitherto unformulated piece of information constitutes more of a redirection of the informational process than feeding back to the patient information already expressed. We realize, of course, that the difference in the value of the therapist informational stimuli may be less between categories (4) and (5) than between, let us say, categories (3) and (4). The system of categories does not seem to constitute a linear scale.

CATEGORY (6)

Definition: The therapist introduces a *sequence* of new propositions.

Description: The therapist actively reorganizes informational propositions already conveyed. Propositions classified here will be recognized as "interpretative" propositions. In our view, the informational stimulus value of such "interpretative" propositions is that they recombine in a new way the information given or potentially available, and thus tend to *redirect* the flow of subsequent patient information. To put it another way, the therapist manipulates information made available to him by the patient, places that information into a new framework, and confronts the patient with it with the purpose of having the patient's further communications be relevant to such a restructured informational field. To illustrate fully the context in which interpretative propositions are used by therapists would require the presentation of long sequences. However, only one brief excerpt is presented here.

Illustration:

Therapist: It seems to me that you have had a rather strong reaction to the way you were brought up, I think that you missed a home. And you missed it a great deal. And I think that in a way, that in a certain sense, that became the central fact of your life, that you had been abandoned as it were.

CATEGORY (7)

Definition: The therapist introduces a specific proposition with the intention of soliciting a particular item of information.

Description: Therapist propositions falling into this category are, in our view, actually intended to obtain a specific bit of information and often require a "yes" or "no" response.

Illustration:

Patient: There was an older brother.
Therapist: How much older than you was he? Category (7)

Patient: I was surprised at finding myself not as strong as I felt.
Therapist: This was after the operation? Category (7)

CATEGORY (8)

Definition: The therapist *excludes* a specific topic or proposition as a subject for communication.

Description: Propositions falling into this category are intended to focus patient communications away from the subject matter of preceding communication. However, the topic or proposition to which he is redirected is not given.

Illustration:

Therapist: Let's not go into this right now. Category (8)

Therapist: We do not need the second dream for this session. Category (8)

DESCRIPTION OF PATIENT INFORMATIONAL BEHAVIOR

In describing patient informational behavior, the focus of attention was different from that used in classifying therapist informational behavior. Since an essential element in the therapist role is to stimulate the production of information by patients, therapist informational behavior was classified in terms of the way in which it affected patients' responses (informational stimulus value). However, the patient's informational output was treated as an *outcome* of therapist stimulation, and was classified in terms of the quantity and type of information produced. The *amount* of information in a patient's statement was estimated by counting the number of propositions it contained. Thus a long statement by a patient would be regarded as containing more information than a short statement.

GRAMMATICAL FORM OF COMMUNICATION

Each proposition was classified as to its grammatical form, or mood, as (1) declarative, (2) imperative, or (3) interrogatory. The grammatical form of a proposition communicates information. For example, the use of the question form supplies information as to who is expected to speak, and thus clarifies communicational expectations. Questions are devices by which communication processes may be initiated or set into motion. They are also an extremely effective way of turning the initiative over to the other. Questions would therefore be expected to increase in frequency during treatment when it appeared most necessary to initiate or to maintain the communication process, or to turn the initiative over to the other. The burden of responsibility for such activities ordinarily falls upon the therapist. This is especially true when a patient is having difficulty talking and strain appears in the communication processes. Bales [13] reported that the proportion of questions in problem-solving sessions with which the group members afterwards expressed dissatisfaction was higher than in the sessions with which the group members were satisfied.

AFFECTIVE CONTENT OF COMMUNICATION

The content of each proposition of either a patient or a therapist was coded as to (1) whether it expressed or referred to feeling, (2) whether it clearly did not express or refer to feeling, or (3) whether its affective content was not determinable.

Verbal communication about affect is regarded as a basic feature of psychotherapeutic interactions, and therapists frequently seek to get their patients to verbalize about feelings. Patient affective propositions refer to their feelings (love, fear, pleasure, sadness, etc.).

Some illustrations of patient affective propositions are:

"I felt very hostile . . ."

"I was glad that she wrote to me."

Therapists themselves very rarely discuss their own feelings; hence, when therapist propositions refer to affect they take a somewhat different form from those of patients. Therapist propositions were categorized as affective when they were directed toward eliciting patient affect.

Some illustrations of therapist affective propositions are:

"Tell me why you are crying."

"You felt sad."

"Resented whom?"

Examples of patient non-affective propositions are:

"I went to the movies."

"I was at the museum yesterday."

Examples of therapist non-affective propositions are:

"How long were you working there?"

"When you say this girl, which girl?"

INTERACTION PROCESS CATEGORIES

Bales has developed a system of classification which permits the scoring of every interaction in terms of one of twelve categories. As he says, "this classification still does not catch 'content' in the usual sense of the term when 'content' is usually taken to mean the 'subject matter'; that is, the reference of the symbols used is the interaction, in short 'what' is being talked about. Our method tries to classify rather what we might call the 'process significance' of the single interaction; that is, the 'pragmatic' significance of each act in relation to prior acts and acts expected to come." [14]

We condensed six of the Bales' categories into three, in line with a suggestion made by Zetterberg.[15] The categories used follow: [16, 17]

(1) *Descriptive Propositions* ask for or convey information. They give or ask for orientation, repetition, or clarification.

Examples: "I see that it is six o'clock."

"What does the statement refer to?"

(2) *Evaluative Propositions* ask for or convey appraisal or statements of value. They give or ask for opinions, expression of feeling, or analysis.

Examples: "What do you think is wrong with you?"

"That's fine."

(3) *Prescriptive Propositions* express or ask for directives. They give or ask for suggestions.

Examples: "I would prefer that you didn't."
"Where should we begin?"

FRAME OF REFERENCE OR ROLE SYSTEM

The dimension of information discussed in this section differs in emphasis from those of quantity, form, intended stimulus value, and affective direction described earlier. We are now concerned in a limited sense with *what* the proposition refers to, with what it is about. Our emphasis now is in classifying communication as referring to the various systems or role relationships in which the patient participates. We are particularly concerned here with identifying propositions in which the therapist or the patient discuss their roles and expectations with regard to therapy. It was assumed that one of the ways in which a patient "learns" about his own and the therapist's roles is through the references which the therapist makes to these roles, that is through role information provided by the therapist. The subject matter of each proposition was therefore classified in terms of the following frames of references:

(1) *Primary System* (the treatment). Included in this category are patient or therapist propositions that refer to their roles during treatment and the process of therapy, and to the purposes, goals, and accomplishments of therapy.

Examples:

Therapist: There's no homework, no reference work, it's all done here.

Therapist: Talk about it anyway even though you think it's unimportant.

Therapist: Could you just take a moment to tell me what the specific areas are in which there has been help?

Patient: Isn't a therapist able to tell me a thing like this?

Patient: I want to be cured.

Patient: Was there some misunderstanding about the appointment time?

(2) *Secondary System.* Included in this category are propositions in which the manifest content refers to therapist and patient in other than their primary roles as patient and therapist. Transference phenomena readily fall into this category.

Examples:

Therapist: Are you projecting doing to me what you did to your father?
Therapist: I'm not angry with you.

Patient: I want you to treat me as a child.
Patient: I was thinking of asking you out to dinner.

(3) *Tertiary Systems.*

a. The Family. Included in this category are propositions that refer directly to the patient's status in the family system.

Examples:

Therapist: What did your father say about this?
Therapist: Your brother was trying to make you jealous.

Patient: I remember talking to my father like this.
Patient: Sex with my husband is not very enjoyable.

b. Other Social Systems. Included in this category are propositions that refer to specific social systems other than the family. The actual person or group must be mentioned.

Examples:

Therapist: Why do you feel that way about this girl?
Therapist: You think he doesn't like you.

Patient: The boss complimented me.
Patient: I was trying to bind her close to me.

(4) *The Self.* Included in this category are references to life experiences past and present that do not refer directly to other reference systems.

Examples:

Therapist: You feel depressed.
Therapist: How many years ago did it happen?

Therapist: Well, there's some basis for your feeling.
Therapist: Did you enjoy the concert?

Patient: I am always playing hero.
Patient: At this time, I feel secure and without anxiety.

CONTINUITY OR CONSISTENCY OF FRAME OF REFERENCE

A desirable characteristic of therapeutic informational exchanges, or for that matter of all communication, is the appropriateness of the reply or feedback. A reply is deemed appropriate if it is responsive or relevant. One way of approximating the relevance of a patient's response to a therapist's remark is to ascertain if it is drawn from the same subject matter area or system of role relationships as is the therapist's remark. Continuance of the terms of reference by the patient constitutes a sort of consensual validation of effective communication between therapist and patient, because it signifies that at least there is an agreement between them as to *what* they are communicating about. By identifying the reference *category* of a patient's response, it is possible to get a rough estimate of its relevance to the preceding therapist communication. If a patient statement falls into the same reference category as the therapist statement that precedes it, it is treated as evidence that communication regarding a given content is continuing. If it falls into a different category, it is regarded as evidence that a change in subject has been introduced. Frequent shifts in subject matter suggest, among other things, dissatisfaction and lack of consensus on the part of the patient and the therapist as to what to talk about.

We also classified change of subject *within* the patient statement, so that we could assess continuity of subject matter within one continuous patient utterance.

TABLE 1

CATEGORIES USED IN DATA ANALYSIS

Units of Quantity
- (1) Proposition
- (2) Statement
- (3) Exchange

Categories of Informational Specificity
- (1) Passive encouragement
- (2) Active encouragement
- (3) Limits to subject matter area
- (4) Limits to specific old proposition
- (5) Introduces specific new proposition
- (6) Interpretation
- (7) Limits to specific answer
- (8) Excludes discussion

Grammatical Form of Propositions
- (1) Declarative
- (2) Imperative
- (3) Interrogatory

Affective Content of Propositions
- (1) Affective, expresses or refers to feelings
- (2) Non-affective, does not refer to feelings
- (3) Affective content indeterminable

Interaction Process Categories
- (1) Descriptive
- (2) Evaluative
- (3) Prescriptive

Role System Reference Categories
- (1) Primary System
- (2) Secondary System
- (3) Tertiary System
- (4) The Self

NOTES

1. Rogers, *Counseling and Psychotherapy.*
2. Wolberg, *The Technique of Psychotherapy.*
3. Deutsch, *Applied Pschoanalysis.*
4. To provide the reader with more information about the approach of each of the therapists who cooperated in this project, we are presenting some verbatim excerpts from their pre-therapy interviews in which they were asked about their therapeutic role and their conceptions about therapy.

Therapist A: My role in the therapeutic situation is to help the patient. . . . He should feel reassured that he is being treated as a person and not just that his organ is being treated. . . . you must study each patient in terms of his capacity to understand what's going on. . . . the essence of the therapeutic relationship is inherent in the concept that a doctor-patient relationship is a transaction. I don't believe that the doctor treats the patient, or that the patient is treated by the doctor. A relationship is set up in which the doctor plays one role and the patient another, and if this role can be managed successfully, then the patient is helped. It's a very complicated transaction, involving the secretary, the office, the doctor's connections, the patient's cultural attitude toward doctors, his previous history with the therapist; the essence is contained in the word transaction, or interaction.

Therapist B: I see my role as helping the patient to feel better and to function better . . . partly to educate him and partly to free him from restricting ideas that he may have. . . . I try to make myself as accepting and non-punitive and uncritical as possible; I try to give the patient a feeling that I will love him, or at least I will not criticize him regardless of what he may say and feel. . . . I would say that the essence of the therapeutic relationship is mutual trust and love . . . it's not very operational . . . but that's the best I can do . . .

Therapist C: My feeling about the role that a doctor plays in the therapeutic situation is that ideally he should play the role of a mirror and reflect the patient's emotions back to the patient. . . . where a little reassurance or support would be advisable, then I sometimes step out of the role and go ahead and say something that will give the patient support and reassurance . . . . but ideally I try to play . . . a neutral role. . . . My feeling is that the way that therapy is actually accomplished is to work through the transference, either by interpreting the transference to the patient—giving them insight in this way—or allowing the patients to go ahead and verbalize their own feelings about the transference and bring out feelings.

Therapist D: I would say my technique is one of reacting differently to the patient than he has expected in his neurotic distortions . . . Essentially, listening, letting the patient express his own feelings and thoughts so he can declare what is in his mind. . . . The essence of the therapeutic relationship is the transference . . . in the sense that the corrective experience is part of the process of helping.

5. Though from a research point of view it would have been desirable to have had an interview with the patients previous to the beginning of therapy, contact with the patient was limited to obtaining some minimal case history material from him over the telephone. This was done upon the recommendation of the participating therapists, who felt that a research contact prior to therapeutic interaction might create some problems for both therapy and for the research.

6. For a similar point of view, see: Brosin, "Information Theory and Clinical Medicine," *Current Trends in Information Theory.*

7. Bales, *Interaction Process Analysis.*

8. Dollard, "A Method of Measuring Tension in Written Documents," *Journal of Abnormal and Social Psychology,* XLII (1947), 3–32.

9. Murray, "A Content-Analysis Method for Studying Psychotherapy," *Psychological Monographs,* Vol. LXX (1956), No. 13.

10. Lennard, "Studies in Factual Interviewing," ed. by Wiggins and Back, Vol. I.

11. Miller, "Psycholinguistics," *Handbook of Social Psychology,* ed. by Lindzey, p. 701.

12. Slight liberties have been taken with the grammatical form of verbatim material in some of the quotes used here in order to make them more intelligible.

13. Parsons, Bales, and Shils, editors, *Working Papers in the Theory of Action,* p. 116.

14. Bales, letter to Conrad Arensberg, 1950.

15. Zetterberg, *Toward an Action Theory,* unpublished manuscript, 1955.

16. The following rules give detailed coding instructions:

Descriptive Propositions

(a) There should be no doubt involved. Proposition refers to a "fact."
(b) The speaker is in a position to know the fact. Example: "I was angry."
(c) Affect is not considered. If an emotion is described as a fact, it is coded here. See the example in (b).
(d) There should be a minimum of interpretation, analysis, opinion, or inference involved.
(e) General, indeterminate questions are coded here. Examples: "Do you have anything in mind?" and "For instance?"

Evaluative Propositions

(a) If doubt is involved, the proposition is coded here. Examples: "I think . . . ," "It seems . . . ," and ". . . perhaps . . ."
(b) If the speaker is not in a position to know but is only guessing or inferring, the proposition is coded here. Example: "You are upset."
(c) The only kind of affect that is necessarily coded here is the expression of preference, wish, value judgement, etc.
(d) Propositions involving interpretation, analysis, or inference are coded here.
(e) Only questions specifically asking for evaluation, interpretation, analysis, opinion, etc., are coded here.

Prescriptive Propositions

(a) Propositions defining what should or must be done are coded here. Examples: "We will have to stop in a few minutes" and "That's something we must consider, too."
(b) Usually therapist "wishes" imply a prescription for the patient and should be coded here. Example: "I would like to hear it all from you."

17. Our reliability findings confirm those reported by Bales in *Interaction Process Analysis.*

Part Two

THERAPY AS A SYSTEM OF ACTION

CHAPTER III

Differentiation

Section 1. Temporal Differentiation over Therapy

One of the questions of major interest from the very outset of our study was whether temporal differentiation—a uniform patterning of activities over time—would be exhibited by therapeutic interaction; whether changes in some types of actions along the temporal axis reflect requirements of the system rather than the problems, personality, and therapeutic orientations of the particular participants.

"A certain time span is inevitably assumed when one speaks of a system. The system consists of the interaction of units, and this means that some process of action and reaction has to be completed before one can give a description of any state of the system as a whole, or any change of state." [1]

Interaction is a "sequence of qualitatively different activities of human individuals which is distributed in time and between individuals in such a way that seems to be organized and patterned in a great number of ways." [2]

Patterning of interaction through time was explored by Bales and his co-workers by studying single meetings of small problem-solving groups. These researchers developed the concept of phase to describe "qualitatively different sub-periods within total continuous periods of interaction." In Bales' view, the different conditions under which interaction systems may operate result in different types of phase movement.

Yet the occurrence of phase movement, the phenomenon of patterned differentiation over time, was considered to be independent of prior conditions, i.e., the kind of group involved, the reason for its creation, and the characteristics of group members. The existence of some determinate order in action processes over time was concluded to be characteristic of *social* systems. The notion of differentiation had, of course, already been applied to *biological* systems such as human organisms and plants by other scientists.[3]

To investigate uniform patterning of activities over time, Bales turned his attention to experimentally constituted groups which met once for a session of less than two hours duration and were given an artificial problem to solve. While scientists had been implicitly aware that behavior in human relationships can be a function of the length of time the relationship persists, Bales[4] presented systematic, quantitative documentation of this pattern, i.e., a distribution of observed behaviors[5] changing in a uniform fashion from the beginning to the end of an experimental time period. He found that "under the conditions enumerated before, groups tend to move in their interaction from a relative emphasis upon problems of orientation to problems of evaluation and subsequently to problems of control and that concurrent with these transitions the relative frequencies of both negative and positive reactions tend to increase."[6] The development and application of these data based on the study of problem-solving groups led to some important hypotheses about the process of problem-solving.[7] Since a psychotherapy group may be viewed as essentially a problem-solving group, we were intrigued with the possibilities inherent in the concept of differentiation or patterning of activities over time for exploring the character of psychotherapeutic systems. In the traditional view of therapy, behavior is viewed and interpreted in terms of intra-personal rather than interpersonal or interactional variables. Patient behavior is described in terms of psychodynamics (repression, projection, etc.) and therapist behavior is described in terms of therapeutic strategy or tactics. Here then was the challenge —to place system characteristics, rather than traditional concerns with patient and therapist, to the forefront of attention.

As a starting point we hypothesized, therefore, that the therapy situation constitutes an interaction system and consequently exhibits specifiable uniformities such as:

(a) relative movement in the frequency with which certain behaviors (acts) occur. Specifically, there will be a movement from an emphasis upon problems of orientation, to problems of evaluation, and then to problems of control.

(b) Movement in the frequency with which positive and negative interpersonal acts occur will be directly related to the extent with which problems of evaluation and control are dealt with in the therapy interaction.

In addition to looking for patterns of differentiation according to the "Bales Categories," we examined all of the variables included in the research for systematic changes over time. Among the variables examined in this connection were: primary system communication, that is, communication revolving around reciprocal rights and duties of therapist and patient in their therapist-patient roles; affective communication, that is, communication expressing or directed toward the patient's feelings; number of questions asked by therapist or patient; certain quantitative ratios of therapist and patient activity; informational characteristics of communication; etc.

Therapy exhibits a "system within a system" character. Therapy as a whole, the total life of the relationship between therapist and patient, constitutes a system. This system consists of subunits (sessions), each of which can also be considered as a system. Thus one could look for a patterning of variables during each session as well as over therapy as a whole. This means that in addition to raising the question of whether therapist and patient communication is in some respects uniformly patterned over time—irrespective of the particular therapist and patient involved and irrespective of the patient's problem or the therapist's ideology—we may also examine the relationship between the differentiation occurring during therapy as a whole and that occurring within the limits of each hour.

DIFFERENTIATION OVER THE FIRST EIGHT MONTHS OF PSYCHOTHERAPY

Patterning in Interaction Process Variables Over Time. Since our transcribed psychotherapy data were scored for the Bales Interaction Process categories, it was possible to deal with the question of whether the kind of behavioral differentiation which was found to occur in the problem-solving groups studied by Bales was also exhibited by our psychotherapy groups. It seemed plausible that, to the extent that the psychotherapy situation constitutes a genuine interaction system with a problem-solving emphasis, a similar type of differentiation would appear in it.

For example, one might hypothesize that when a problem is dealt with over a period of time, the initial sessions would emphasize orientation and the later sessions would focus on evaluative behavior.

The reader should take note of the two senses in which Bales makes use of the notion of problem: "From my microscopic point of view all interaction process has a problem-solving direction, whether the people are trying to solve what we might call a substantive problem or not. The categories are differentiated from each other by their different relations to a problem-solving sequence but the 'problems' involved are problems of interacting together and communicating. The fact that interaction consists of attempts at problem-solving does not at all imply that people solve their substantive problems." [8]

Analysis of our psychotherapy data revealed that the patterning of therapist behavior over the life (or early life) of therapy was indeed similar to that of the participants in the problem-solving groups studied by Bales. Figure 1 shows that therapist behavior characterized as orientation (asking for and

FIGURE 1

PATTERNS OF TEMPORAL DIFFERENTIATION OVER 50 SESSIONS OF THERAPY: THERAPIST ORIENTATIVE AND EVALUATIVE PROPOSITIONS

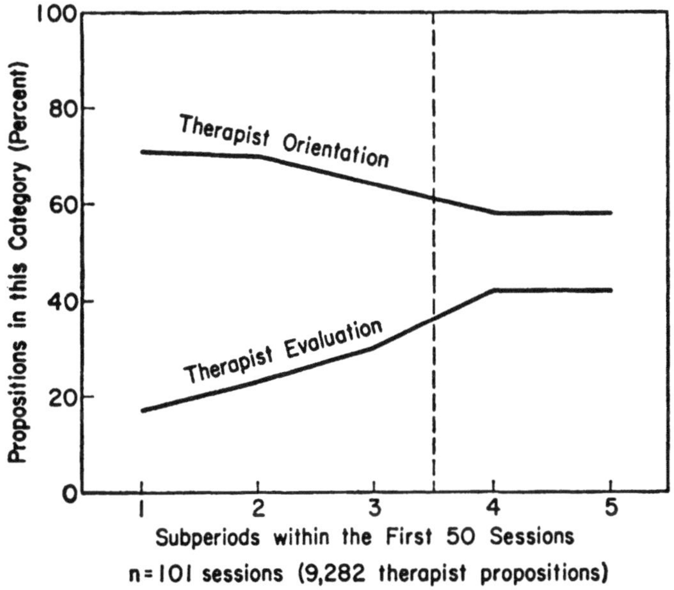

The five subperiods are (1) sessions 1–3; (2) sessions 4–6; (3) sessions 7–8; (4) sessions from the third and fourth months of therapy; and (5) sessions from the fourth through the seventh months of therapy. The vertical broken line on the graph calls attention to the fact that the later two groups of sessions are not consecutive with the earlier sessions.

giving repetitions, clarifications, and confirmations) decreases through the first fifty hours of therapy, while evaluative behavior (asking for and giving opinions, evaluations, analyses, and expression of feeling) increases and then appears to reach a plateau.[9]

While the pattern of differentiation exhibited by our therapists appears to be similar to that of the participants in the Bales groups, the amount of behavior falling into given categories at any subperiod (group of sessions) was different. Therapists exhibit a higher percentage of orienting behavior than do members of the Bales groups, and though the amount of therapist communication devoted to orientation decreases by the fiftieth session, it is still considerably higher than that reported by Bales for his groups.[10]

This difference may be functionally specific to the therapeutic group. The substantive problem that the therapeutic group is attacking is the patient's "disorientation" itself. Not only does the therapist face the usual problems of orientation inherent in any problem-solving interaction, but also the additional problem of overcoming the patient's disorientation and uncertainty.

Transference manifestations in therapy imply that patient expectations of the therapist are not appropriate and cannot be fulfilled by him. These expectations need to be revised constantly by the therapist, and the patient has to be reoriented over and over again before a more realistic adaptation is established.

In general, the patient's "problem" can be conceived of as a deficit in ability to perceive and respond properly and adequately to his environment. Consequently a greater amount of orientation is required to compensate for this deficit. The patient's role in therapy is a difficult and unusual one, and a great deal of information and orientation is required to enable the patient to function properly in the patient role.

Differentiation in *patient* behavior through time, as characterized by the Bales categories, is less consistent. There *is* a slight decrease in orientation (Table 2) and a slight increase in evaluative behavior (Table 3), for the group as a whole. The pattern is somewhat more consistent when we compare the first eight sessions with the later sessions.

We found that the pattern of differentiation among the therapists was more consistent than among the patients, and was more nearly analogous to that of the participants in problem-solving groups. We would like to offer several ideas in connection with this finding:

(a) The therapist conceives of his role as involving differentiated action, i.e., one does different things at different times. Specific actions make sense to him only in relation to the total configuration of actions required by his job.

(b) The difference between the differentiation patterns of therapist and patient is due to the fact that while the patient is discouraged from engaging in precisely those activities that characterize the behavior of individuals in problem-solving groups, the therapist is far more goal-directed and in conscious control. In problem-solving groups, negative sanctions are imposed by the participants upon each other for inconsistent, nonrational, and illogical communication. On the other hand, to accomplish important goals of analytic treatment (i.e., to bring unconscious partial processes to the surface) therapists discourage patients from engaging in "rationalizing" behavior (i.e., using reason to integrate what seems illogical or inappropriate) and instead encourage them to allow their unacceptable and inconsistent feelings and thoughts to emerge.

(c) The therapist participates in a large number of therapeutic systems in contrast to the patient's participation in only one such setting. He is therefore apt to be more sensitive to the system requirements of the therapeutic problem-solving group.

Differentiation in Primary System References over Time. Basic to our view of psychotherapy is our attitude that it involves a process of socialization or learning whereby certain role behaviors are acquired. Such a socialization process should reflect itself in a differentiation of the activities of the participants over time during the course of therapy. In this section, we will describe one important aspect of the socialization process.

A parent teaches his child about what is and what is not expected of him, and what he may or may not expect of his parent. Such socializing information may be elicited upon inquiry by the child, may be the result of the child's disappointment of a parental expectation, or may come quite unsolicited

FIGURE 2

PATTERNS OF TEMPORAL DIFFERENTIATION OVER 50 SESSIONS OF THERAPY: THERAPIST AND PATIENT PRIMARY SYSTEM PROPOSITIONS

See Fig. 1 for specification of the five subperiods.

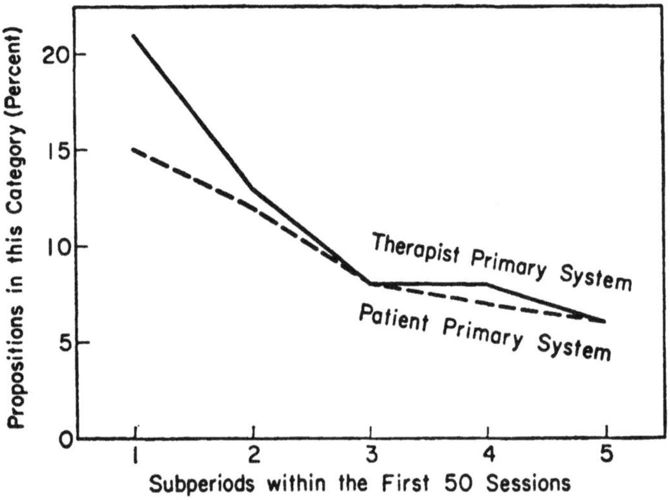

from the parent. Similarly, we conceive it to be an essential characteristic of a therapeutic relationship that a patient be informed about what is or is not expected of therapists and patients and thus be "socialized into the patient role." We have already discussed the importance of this induction not only for the patient's performance in the therapeutic relationship but also for the patient's general ability to function within a variety of other role relationships.

The discussion of the requirements, obligations, rights, and duties of therapists and patients and the goals, purposes, and accomplishments of therapy were called communications about the "primary system." When we examined psychotherapeutic communication from the point of view of system referent, we discovered that there was a very consistent downward trend, over the life of therapy, in the frequency of primary system references (see Fig. 2). The decrease was of considerable magnitude, dropping to less than one-half of the original amount by the fourth month of treatment. In other words, as therapy progressed, discussion about therapy itself and the reciprocal therapist-patient roles decreased.

Of course, role communication at the manifest verbal level does not by any means exhaust the possible ways by which role information is transmitted to a patient. But there is probably a high degree of redundancy and eventually most nonverbal messages are encoded into words, so there is undoubtedly some correlation between verbal and nonverbal cues. At this stage of the game, unfortunately, the only way we could attempt to measure role learning directly and systematically was by counting the number of direct verbal references to the primary system.

Although we do not present the specific data, it is worth mentioning in passing that the decrease in discussion of the therapist-patient relationship is not paralleled by a decrease in the discussion of other role relationships, e.g., patient role as family member or as an employee. Actually, communication about the patient's various role sets constitutes a continuing concern of therapeutic communication.

The decrease in communication about the primary role system occurs for our study group as a whole and appears as a trend in every one of the eight therapist-patient pairs. It reflects the inevitability of socialization as a consequence of psychotherapy irrespective of the orientation and skill of the therapist and the psychological problem of the patient. To resolve the problem of what a patient may expect and what may be expected of him appears to be an indispensable requisite for maintaining the therapeutic system from one session to the next. We would guess that, without at least minimal resolution of this problem, continuation of the therapeutic process would become impossible. We believe that at least some well-known practical problems in therapeutic practice (e.g., high drop-out rate in clinics where psychotherapy is carried on with patients from low socio-economic groups) may be related to failure to sufficiently socialize patients to their role so that they could function within the definitions provided by the therapists or by the institutions concerned.

In addition to discussions of the therapist in the status of therapist, a great deal of communication during psychotherapy refers to the therapist as a substitute for important figures in the patient's life, i.e., in transference roles. Communications of this kind were coded in a separate category and do not decrease during therapy.

The Patterning of Affective Communications. Concomitant with the decrease in discussion about therapist-patient role expectations, both the therapist and the patient tend to increase their communications about affect (see Fig. 3). This means that, as therapy proceeded, the therapists increased the frequency with which their propositions inquired into and solicited patient verbalization about feelings, and also that our patients began to verbalize more voluminously about feelings. The inverse movement of primary system communication and affective communication over time is not incidental to but derives from the very nature of the therapeutic task. Precisely one of the things the patient learns about his role as a patient is to put his thoughts and especially his feelings into words. Though not all therapists would formulate it this way, we believe most would subscribe to Sullivan's statement to the effect that: "One has information about one's experiences only to the extent that one has tended to communicate it to another . . ." [11]

Some might say that the mobilization or freeing of affect per se, for example, affect which has been previously held in check by inappropriate fears, is also one of the important aims of the therapeutic relationship. To that end not only verbalization of feeling but merely experiencing feelings is encouraged.

FIGURE 3
PATTERNS OF TEMPORAL DIFFERENTIATION OVER 50 SESSIONS OF THERAPY: THERAPIST AND PATIENT AFFECTIVE PROPOSITIONS

See Fig. 1 for specification of the five subperiods.

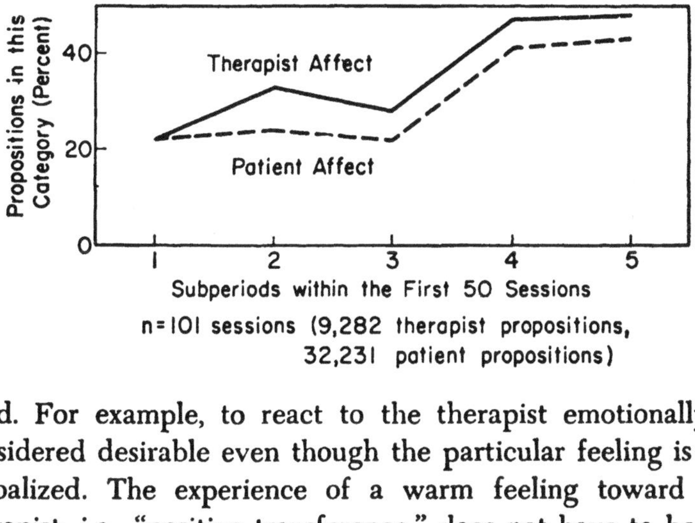

n=101 sessions (9,282 therapist propositions, 32,231 patient propositions)

aged. For example, to react to the therapist emotionally is considered desirable even though the particular feeling is not verbalized. The experience of a warm feeling toward the therapist, i.e., "positive transference," does not have to be expressed verbally in order to be of value to the patient.

Yet a therapist explicitly teaches his patient to put his feelings into words [12] while implicitly moving his patient in this direction by making emotion the target of his own references. As the therapist increases his interest and inquiry into feelings, thus documenting their validity for the patient, the patient increases his own discussion of them. The very interesting interrelation over time between therapist and patient affective communication will be the subject of a more detailed discussion in Chapter IV.

The elicitation of patient affect is widely regarded as an important task of psychotherapy. A uniform increase over time in concern with affective communication was shown in our study group. This result shows once again that differentiation exhibited by the psychotherapeutic system follows logically from the special tasks of the therapeutic group and their implementation. It is only surprising that differentiation is manifested so clearly and consistently by our therapist-patient pairs.

Pattern of Interaction. Each statement made by a therapist may be regarded as a therapeutic act or intervention. Each interaction (an exchange of statements) therefore includes one therapist intervention. The number of exchanges per hour or per transcribed page gives us the *rate of interaction* which measures the *frequency* with which therapist and patient communications follow upon one another.

For our study group as a whole (more precisely, for six of the eight therapist-patient pairs), the interaction rate remains fairly constant during the first eight sessions of treatment and then drops during the later sessions of therapy (see Table 4). In other words, therapists intervene more frequently during the early sessions of treatment than during later sessions.

What does this decrease in the rate of interaction mean? It could indicate that socialization of the patient is proceeding successfully, so that on the one hand the patient is acting more in line with the therapist's expectations and the therapist does not feel called upon to intervene so frequently, and that on the other hand, the patient has become more knowledgeable in his role as patient and thus calls upon the therapist to intervene less frequently.

Pattern of Therapist Informational Structuring. As therapy proceeds, therapist communications tend to become more highly specific. Such nonspecific communications as "Mm-hm" and "Yes, please go on" decrease in frequency during the early sessions of therapy and become relatively infrequent thereafter. Since each "Mm-hm," etc., was counted as an intervention, perhaps the decrease in frequency of nonspecific therapist interventions of this kind over time partly accounts for the parallel decrease in interaction rate previously reported.

The frequency with which therapist statements of high informational specificity occur increases from the first stage of therapy (sessions 1–3) to the second stage (sessions 4–6), stays at a high level thereafter, and shows no tendency to increase over time (see Table 5). After the therapist passes through the initial phases of establishing communicational rapport, he maintains an informationally highly specific mode of communication throughout the remainder of therapy, varying only slightly in degree of specificity from session to session. Once patient communication acquires a momentum of its own, it can move ahead without the encouragement offered by noncommittal and unstructured therapist feedback.

Section 2. Temporal Differentiation Within the Session

The original Bales observations on phase movement were made with single problem-solving sessions as the focus of observation. In the Bales and Parsons view, interaction over time per se implies some kind of patterned and uniform unfolding of activity on the part of participants. A question of particular interest is whether the type of differentiation observed over the longer time periods of therapeutic interaction is similar to that observed during more limited time periods such as the length of one therapeutic session; in other words, insofar as differentiation is concerned, does the single session represent a miniature of therapy as a whole or do variations in the length of the interaction between participants eventuate in variations between the macro- and micropatterns of differentiation?

TABLE 2

PROPORTION OF PATIENT PROPOSITIONS THAT WERE ORIENTATIVE FOR EACH OF FIVE SUBPERIODS[a]

	1	2	3	4	5
Orientative	.73	.77	.72	.72	.68

n = 101 sessions (32,231 patient propositions)

[a] See Fig. 1 for description of the five subperiods.

TABLE 3

PROPORTION OF PATIENT PROPOSITIONS THAT WERE EVALUATIVE FOR EACH OF FIVE SUBPERIODS

	1	2	3	4	5
Evaluative	.26	.22	.28	.28	.34

n = 101 sessions (32,231 patient propositions)

TABLE 4

AVERAGE NUMBER OF INTERACTIONS PER PAGE FOR EACH OF FIVE SUBPERIODS

	1	2	3	4	5
Interactions	4.6	4.6	4.9	3.9	3.4

n = 101 sessions (1,282 pages)

TABLE 5

PROPORTION OF THERAPIST PROPOSITIONS WITH HIGH INFORMATIONAL SPECIFICITY[a] FOR EACH OF FIVE SUBPERIODS

	1	2	3	4	5
High Specificity	.54	.69	.60	.63	.63

n = 101 sessions (9,282 therapist propositions)

[a] Informational Categories 5 through 8

The data on phase movement within the session were obtained by dividing each session into three time intervals of equal length. Thus a 45-minute session would be divided into three phases of fifteen minutes each. Comparisons were then made among the three intervals. The third, fifth, and seventh sessions of therapy for seven patients were so treated. The specific categories were then counted and percentaged for each time period.[13]

SIMILARITIES BETWEEN PATTERNING OF THE SESSION AND OF THERAPY

Most striking among the similarities between movement of communication in the individual session and movement during the first fifty sessions of therapy is the decrease of primary system communications on the part of therapist and patient within the individual session. In other words, primary role communication is more frequent at the beginning of each hour than toward the end (Fig. 5).

It appears as if induction into the patient role is a task which frequently has to be resumed at the beginning of each session. It is only after some discussion of the therapist-patient primary relationship that the patient can once again assume the patient role. During the second phase of the hour, primary system information decreases by more than one-half, and by the third phase it is only one-eighth as much as it was during the beginning of the session. Thus a large proportion of the decrease in primary system communication which occurs over therapy as a whole (the first fifty sessions) may be attributed to a progressive decrease in the amount of therapist-patient role system discussion at the outset of each session. We are reminded here of the classical learning curve.

Our data also suggest that if the patient has been absent for a time, primary system communication is almost indispensable for his resocialization into the requirements of the

PATTERNS OF TEMPORAL DIFFERENTIATION WITHIN THE SESSION

FIGURE 4
INTERACTION PROCESS CATEGORIES (BALES)

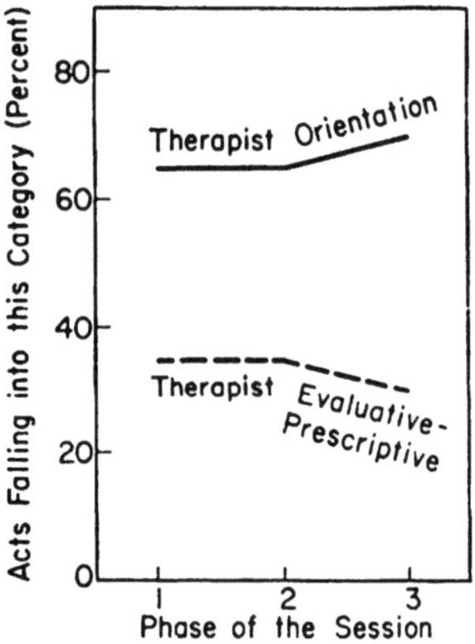

n = 21 sessions (1,752 therapist propositions)

FIGURE 5
PRIMARY SYSTEM COMMUNICATION

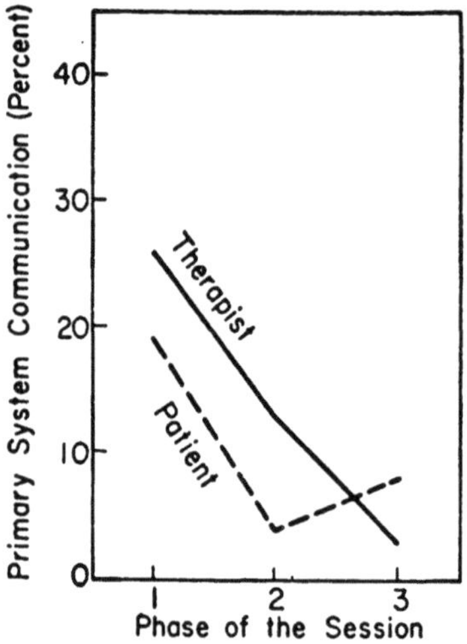

n = 21 sessions (1,752 therapist propositions, 3,425 patient propositions)

FIGURE 6
AFFECTIVE COMMUNICATION

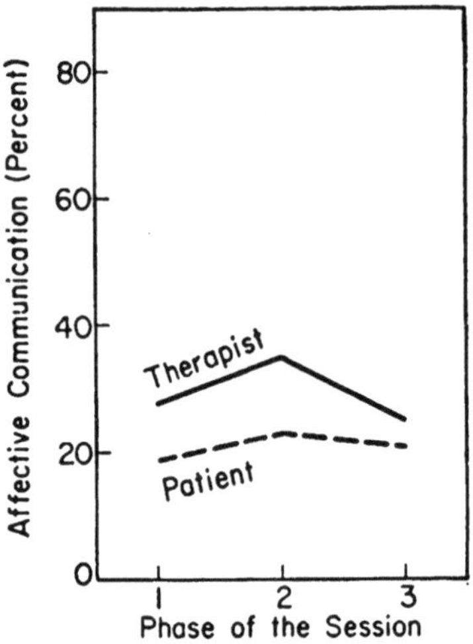

n = 21 sessions (1,752 therapist propositions, 3,425 patient propositions)

therapeutic relationship. Freud comments on the "Monday crust,"[14] the return of resistances and regression during psychoanalysis each time that treatment is interrupted by the weekend. Yet, less and less of this resocialization appears to be necessary as therapy progresses. One might speculate that just as there is in successive sessions a decrease in the amount of effort required to resocialize the patient into the therapeutic relationship, there might be a concurrent lessening of the effort required on the part of the patient for his reinduction into the variety of other role relationships in which he takes part.

From the first to the second phase of an individual session, just as was the case over the life of therapy, decrease in primary system communication is accompanied by an increase in communication about affect (see Fig. 6). This increase is attributable to the fact that therapists sharply increase their attention to affect from the first to the second phase of the session. The findings with regard to patients are less consistent. When we examined their affective communication we found that affective communication is highest in the second phase for only four out of our seven patients and lowest for one.

We suspect that our failure to find that affective communication increases progressively toward the end of the session, as it does for therapy as a whole, is due to the fact that toward the end of a therapy session there often occurs considerable talk about appointment times, fees, etc., which by definition is scored as non-affective communication. This automatically lowers the percentage of affective propositions and introduces an artifact into our data.

Another hypothesis is that the exploration of affect in a therapeutic session is in connection with a theme introduced in the first phase of the session. Affective expression about the theme occurs in the second phase and by the last phase of the session both the patient and the therapist, realizing the session is coming to an end, prepare themselves by withdrawing to relatively less affect-laden topics.

Therapists often find that important new material is brought up at the end of the session. But since this can be interpreted as a maneuver on the part of the patient not to deal with this important material, since by design he does not leave enough time to cope with it, it is not surprising that our results do not show a rise in affect toward the end of the session.

The informational specificity of therapist communications tends to increase from the first to the second phase of the session (see Table 6). In this increase in structuring, we see another corollary to the long-term increase in informational specificity which occurs very early in the life of therapy, that is, from the first to the second subperiod. In the individual session, it also appears early. Nondirective and diffuse comments by the therapist ease the patient into topics of his own choosing, and after the patient has begun to verbalize, the therapist's comments become informationally more specific. However, within the individual session, we found that a decrease in informational specificity occurred after the second phase of the session in four out of the seven cases. In this respect, the pattern for the individual session seems to differ from the pattern for longer periods of therapy.

DISSIMILARITY BETWEEN THE SESSION AND THERAPY

The phase movement within the individual session, as assessed by means of the Bales Interaction Process Categories, did not replicate the long-term trend and thus did not resemble the pattern found by Bales in his small one-session problem-solving groups. The emergent picture of phase movement within the session is almost the reverse of that postulated—although it appears to exhibit its own time-contingent order and pattern (see Fig. 4).

For example, while it would have been expected that orienting behavior would be highest in the first phase of the session, we found that for the patients—with one exception—orienting behavior was *lowest* in the first phase. On the other hand, while orienting behavior in the first phase of the session is not *consistently* lowest for the therapist, in only one case is it highest for that interval. This result is contrary to what one would expect from the hypothesis of similarity in phase movement.

Movement in behavior devoted to orientation, evaluation, and control is viewed by Bales in relation to the problem-solving sequence. For example, behavior devoted to control (prescriptive actions in our system) are more needed toward the end of the problem-solving sequence than at the beginning.

Our data suggest that the individual session in psychotherapy does not constitute an entire problem-solving sequence in the Bales sense. Our coding conventions might have tended to obscure the pattern somewhat, because the discussion of time and place of future sessions was coded as orienting. This increased the amount of orienting behavior coded for therapist and patient during the end phase.

It should be admitted, however, that the lack of similarity within the individual session between the pattern of differentiation exhibited by primary system communication categories and that exhibited by interaction process categories is somewhat puzzling, in the light of their congruent movement during the first eight months of therapy.

The long term pattern of differentiation in the rate of interaction is not replicated in miniature by the individual session. While in the later sessions of therapy the pace of interaction was *less* rapid than in the earlier sessions, for the individual session it is in the middle phase that the rate of interaction is lowest (see Table 7).

Communication during the middle phase of the session apparently requires the least amount of therapist intervention. Interestingly enough, however, the average duration of silences increases from phase to phase for the patients of all of the therapists.

We would have expected the number of silences to vary concurrently with interaction rate (which is lowest in the middle interval), since in general we found that silences promote therapist intervention. However, something else may be involved here. Apparently silences in the first phase of the session are more often taken by the therapist as a sign of inability on the part of the patient to proceed with verbalization. In the middle phase, which constitutes the core of the session, the therapist tends to be willing to wait longer and to let the patient's feelings emerge at his leisure.

PATTERNS UNIQUE TO THE SESSION

The use of questions has been regarded with special interest in our research. Since a question is a mechanism used to accelerate blocked communication and also to define who has the responsibility for verbalization, it may be considered a basic instrument of communication. While earlier work with published transcripts led us to expect a definite pattern of differentiation in the distribution of questions during therapy, no such long-term pattern was found. However, a long-term cyclical fluctuation in frequency of questions could have been obscured when the data were averaged for three-session intervals.

When the individual session is taken as the unit, a definite trend in the distribution of questions is apparent. Therapist questions are more frequent in the last phase of the session, while for half of the cases there is almost no difference in the frequency of questions between the first and the second phase (see Table 8).

The upsurge of questions in the third phase of the session

TABLE 6

PROPORTION OF THERAPIST PROPOSITIONS OF HIGH INFORMATIONAL SPECIFICITY[a] IN THREE PHASES[b] OF THE SESSION

	Phase 1	*Phase 2*	*Phase 3*
High Specificity	.50	.58	.47

n = 21 sessions (1,752 therapist propositions)

[a] Informational Categories 5 through 8
[b] Each Phase equals one third of the session

TABLE 7

AVERAGE NUMBER OF INTERACTIONS IN THE THREE PHASES OF THE SESSION

	Phase 1	*Phase 2*	*Phase 3*
Interactions	65	54	78

n = 21 sessions (1,282 interactions)

TABLE 8

PROPORTION OF THERAPIST PROPOSITIONS THAT ARE QUESTIONS IN THE THREE PHASES OF THE SESSION

	Phase 1	*Phase 2*	*Phase 3*
Questions	.33	.33	.35

n = 21 sessions (1,752 therapist propositions)

is interpreted as indicating that more strain in communication is experienced by the participants toward the close of the session. The patient is less willing to be the sole communicator at that stage and exerts more pressure to have the therapist intervene, perhaps in the form of interpretation. This conclusion is supported by the increase in silences for the third phase. The therapist is consequently required to redefine communicational expectation with regard to who has the responsibility to verbalize. He does this by returning the initiative to the patient through the use of the question form. This increase in silences may, of course, also be due to a deliberate withholding of questions by the therapist until later in the session.

Section 3. Differentiation of Behavior: Specialization

Like other action systems, psychotherapy systems differentiate along two major axes. Differentiation along the temporal axis has previously been discussed, but the sort of differentiation known as division of labor or specialization still remains to be elucidated. We have also pointed out that in relation to performance (action), degree of differentiation is used synonymously with the nation of asymmetry.

A two-person system such as occurs in psychotherapy may differ from other interpersonal systems (such as friendship pairs) in degree of asymmetry or differentiation. In a friendship relationship, one friend *sometimes* specializes in a different kind of behavior than the other. In a psychotherapy relationship, however, the participants *always* enter with their roles differently defined. Furthermore, the clarity with which the therapist defines his role is considerably greater than that with which the patient defines his.

One may view role differentiation in terms of the role expectations of the participants, or one may study their *actual behavior* (performance) and note the difference in the magnitudes and kinds of communication given. It is the latter which occupies us here (see Fig. 7).

Specialization in behavior is explained in the following:

> Within a given small span of time behavior involves the selection of a given alternative from a larger range of potentialities and allocation of limited resources to the selected alternative. The constriction of resources in this fundamental sense may be said to force a differentiation in the quality of activity in time.[15]

Role specialization in terms of performance implies ". . . patterns which are relatively constant through time . . . repetitive elements . . ." But a question may be raised as to whether the *kind* of specialization involved is a constant one, or one which changes over time.

For the group of patients and therapists we studied, the patients averaged about four times as much verbal material (see Fig. 7) as the therapists. This difference in relative volume of total output remained essentially the same throughout therapy for the group of sessions studied. The patients not only differed from the therapists in terms of their total verbal output for a session or a group of sessions but also, as might be expected, in terms of the average magnitude or extensiveness of single statements. This means that the patient would hold the floor for a considerably greater interval than the therapist. His single verbalizations were on the average about five times as extensive as those of the therapist and at times his contributions were more than a hundred times as extensive.[16] Both therapist and patient verbalizations increased somewhat in extent as therapy proceeded.

In this respect, we see that therapy groups differ from the small problem-solving groups studied by Bales and others. These researchers found more participation by the leaders than by the other group members. Our study shows that the therapist's verbal output is substantially below that of the patient. In addition, we found that the number of therapist questions is

FIGURE 7

ROLE SPECIALIZATION IN EARLY AND LATER SESSIONS

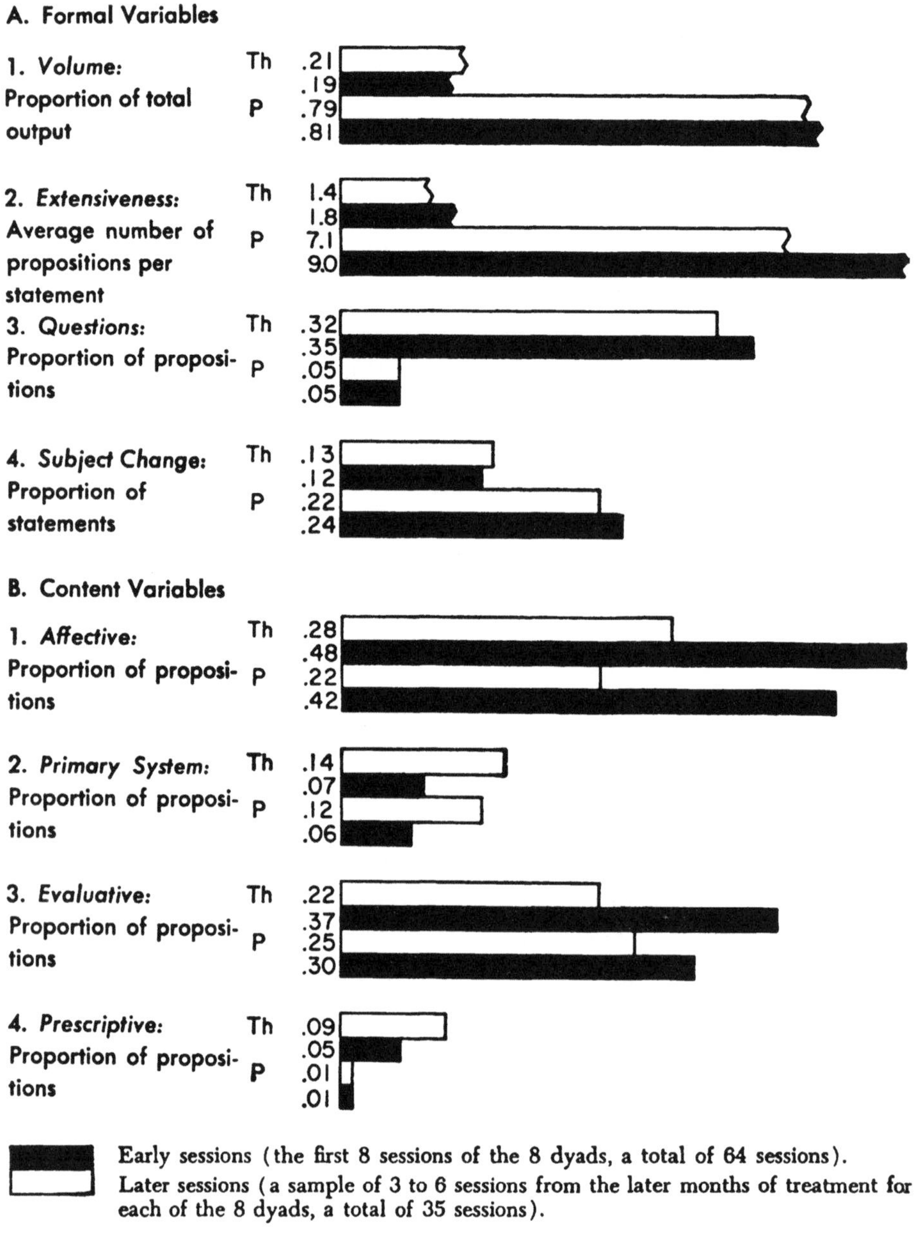

nearly seven times the number of patient questions. Questions are devices for turning the responsibility for communication over to the other partner in a communicational setting. We thus see that the therapist not only specializes in keeping his own communication low, but also in maximizing that of the patient.

With respect to communication about feelings the therapist and the patient—despite the differences in their over-all output—showed rather similar quantitative emphasis. The therapists as a group led the patients slightly in the proportion of communication dealing with affect.[17]

As has been explained, the patterns of therapist and patient affective communication are qualitatively distinct. While the therapist directs the patient to express and to verbalize feelings, he does not discuss his own feelings. The patient, on the other hand, does report on and communicate about his own feelings. Nevertheless, the proportion of both therapist and patient references devoted to feelings increases—almost doubles—for the sample as a whole, from the earlier to the later sessions of treatment. Thus quantitative symmetry in affective communication is maintained (see Fig. 7).[18]

In terms of our view of therapy as a role-learning or socialization process, we note that both therapist and patient devote almost equal amounts of communication to the discussion of therapist-patient role relations (e.g., what behavior is expected from the therapist vis-a-vis the patient, and vice versa). Further, for the study group as a whole, reference by both therapist and patient to their reciprocal role expectations decreases by about one half from the first eight sessions to the later sessions.

The therapist may be considered to be specialized in teaching the patient role. However, this specialization is not reflected as one might expect in a greater concentration upon primary role discussion. Apparently, the patient's concern with obtaining clarity and definition of the patient role is just as salient as the therapist's effort to clarify and define that role. Both participants devote approximately the same amount of output to discussion of the primary system.

Among other findings with regard to action differentiation, it may be of interest to mention a greater patient specialization in communications which change the subject under discussion.

The hypothesis that the therapist would take the initiative in introducing new subject areas [19] and would move discussion away from those he does not consider worthwhile was not borne out. It is the patient who consistently exhibits more subject matter changes both in the early and in the later sessions.

We noted that the general asymmetry between patient and therapist with respect to the formal and quantitative variables (volume, extensiveness, question form, change of subject) remains fairly constant through therapy (see Fig. 7), but the trend toward symmetry exhibited by the content or qualitative categories (affective, primary system, evaluative) increases for the later sessions (see Fig. 7). On the basis of this and other findings available to us, there appears to be a trend toward symmetry when the therapy system is considered. Thus, while the roles of patient and therapist require differentiated activities, their continuous interaction tends to increase the similarity of their behavior.

SUMMARY

1. Patterns of temporal differentiation were identified for the first 50 sessions of therapy and for the individual session.

2. Some variables (primary system communication, affective communication) show a similar temporal patterning for both the macrosystem (therapy) and the microsystem (the session).

3. In general, the phasing of therapist behavior over time is more consistent than that of the patient (with respect to orienting, evaluating, and affective communication).

4. The direction of phasing of therapist behavior (both for the macro- and microsystem) is more similar to that shown by participants in problem-solving groups than is the phasing of patient behavior.

5. Some patterns of differentiation are unique to the session (questions) and others unique to the therapeutic system as a whole (interaction rate).

6. Specialization in therapist and patient verbal behavior is manifested by differences in the quantitative and *formal* aspects of communication (magnitude of verbal output, extensiveness, number of questions, subject change).

7. With respect to the *qualitative* features of communication (primary system, affective, and evaluative communication), therapist and patient behavior is far less differentiated (specialized). This dissymmetry is most pronounced later on in the course of therapy.

NOTES

1. Parsons, Bales, and Shils, *Working Papers in the Theory of Action*, p. 176.

2. Bales, *The Strategy of Small Group Research*.

3. Bertalanffy, "General System Theory," *Life, Language, Law*, ed. by Taylor, p. 58.

> Concepts like those of organization, wholeness, directiveness, teleology, control, self-regulation, differentiation . . . pop up everywhere in the biological, behavioral, and social sciences, and are, in fact, indispensable for dealing with living organisms or social groups.

4. Bales and Strodtbeck, "Phases in Group Problem Solving," *Journal of Abnormal and Social Psychology*, XLVI (September, 1951), 311–22.

5. All acts of group members for a session scored into twelve categories.

6. Bales and Strodtbeck, "Phases in Group Problem Solving," *Journal of Abnormal and Social Psychology*, XLVI (September, 1951), 311–22.

7. Bales, *Interaction Process Analysis*, and Parsons, Bales, and Shils, *Working Papers in the Theory of Action.*

8. Bales, letter to Conrad Arensberg.

9. In order for a variable to be considered to exhibit a uniform patterning over time, it had to exhibit a regular decrease or increase, interval by interval, either for six out of the eight therapist-patient dyads or for three out of the four therapists.

10. a. Also, it was found in an earlier study that therapist evaluative behavior tends to level off comparatively later in the life of the therapy group than in the one-session problem-solving group. See Lennard, *Concepts of Interaction*, 1955.

b. In the analysis of two other separate bodies of therapeutic data, Lennard (*ibid.*) found greater amounts of therapeutic communication devoted to orientation than was found in the Bales groups. Further, in a series of studies of groups to whom psychotomimetic drugs were administered and who were thus experimentally impaired, it was found that more communication revolved around problems of mutual orientation and information than in "ordinary problem solving groups." See Lennard, Jarvik, and Abramson, "Effect of LSD Upon Communication," 1956.

11. Sullivan, *Conceptions of Modern Psychiatry*, p. 90.

12. Two examples of therapists telling their patients to put feelings into words are provided below. They are taken verbatim from our transcripts:

Therapist: Your job here is just to learn how to put your thoughts, your feelings, and your memories into words.

Therapist: Well, the procedure is generally that you lie down and relax on the couch, and then put all your feelings into words, so far as you can.

13. Because of difficulty in establishing comparable time intervals, one therapist-patient pair was not included in this analysis.

14. Freud, "Further Recommendations in the Technique of Psychoanalysis" (1913), *Collected Papers*, II (1949), 347.

Even shorter interruptions have a disconcerting effect on the work; we used to speak jokingly of the "Monday-crust" when we began work again after the rest on Sunday . . .

15. Parsons and Bales, *Family: Socialization and Interaction Process*, p. 264.

16. During the first eight sessions, the mean number of therapist

propositions per exchange was 1.4 while the mean number of patient propositions per exchange was 7.1.

17. During the first eight sessions, the therapists devoted an average of 28 percent of their verbal propositions to affect, while the patients devoted an average of 22 percent to discussing their feelings. During the later sessions, the figure is 48 percent for therapists and 42 percent for patients.

18. Similarity in this area resides in the interdependence between therapist and patient affective references. This is explored in some detail in Chapter IV.

19. When in this chapter we speak of subject change, we are referring to a change in the system of social relations discussed by the therapist and patient. For a description of the categorization of references as referring to one of eight systems of social relations, see Chapter II.

CHAPTER IV

Interdependence of Therapist and Patient Verbal Behavior

One kind of interdependence of behavior occurring in social systems which is of interest to sociologists is the trend toward similarity in performance or orientation. As Homans puts it, "The more frequently persons interact with one another, the more alike in some respects both their activities and their sentiments tend to become." [1] And as Newcomb says, "There is in fact, no social phenomenon which can be more commonly observed than the tendency of freely communicating persons to resemble one another in orientation towards objects of common concern." [2]

We wanted to learn whether or not interacting individuals become more alike in the course of psychotherapy, and if so, with respect to which communicational variables.

Traditional theories of psychotherapy have always maintained the view that the patient, like Peer Gynt, should become more "himself" in the course of therapy, rather than be transformed into a facsimile of the therapist. Our findings (with respect to specific aspects of therapist and patient communication patterns) can be interpreted as bearing out Homans's hypothesis that interacting individuals tend to become more alike as time passes. But whether this means that the patient tends to become more like his therapist as treatment continues or is merely internalizing the communicational patterns he observes during treatment will depend upon how much of a therapist's behavior during treatment is a role he is playing and how much of it truly represents himself. To the extent that a therapist "is himself" (i.e., expresses his own values, preferences, etc.) during treatment, a patient may indeed grow to resemble him; but to the extent that the therapist is not "himself," the patient would merely incorporate those aspects of the therapist's behavior characteristic of the role assumed by him in the particular therapy.

Our results bear on this controversy only indirectly, since communication content was not analyzed directly in relation to specific values and orientation.[3] We did not code our material in terms of similarity in actual values expressed, but only as to whether or not the participants' communication was centered on the same subject or the same mode of communication. One can nevertheless hold that similarity in *what* and *how* one communicates does bear on the question of similarity in values.

The first step in investigating these questions was to examine the natural unit, the therapeutic session. Correlations between given types of therapist and patient verbal behavior were computed. Specifically, correlations were computed between percentage of therapist propositions and percentages of patient propositions which were of the same kind, that is, which were classified in the same category. This was done for three aspects of communication. We are using the term "similarity" to express the fact of an increasing correlation over time between patient and therapist with respect to the following three kinds of communicative sets: (1) primary system references, (2) evaluative communications, and (3) affective communications.

(1) Primary system references, it will be remembered, deal with reciprocal therapist-patient role relations. They revolve around the obligations and activities of therapist and patient

vis-a-vis each other. These references frequently consist of discussions of the purposes of therapy. Primary system references sometimes constitute more than half of all therapist communications during the initial hours of therapy but by the tenth hour of therapy may comprise less than 20 percent of all therapist communications. This is a critical area during the early period of therapy. The exchange of communications between therapist and patient regarding their respective roles is one avenue through which the patient "learns" the patient role and is enabled to function within it.

(2) Evaluative propositions are those which give or ask for appraisals or statements of value. This category covers two of the Bales Interaction Process categories. It was felt that evaluation of behavior was an especially recurrent feature of therapy and that, therefore, tendencies toward similarities in the trends of therapist and patient verbal behavior would have an opportunity to emerge and could be assessed.

(3) Affective propositions are those which are directed toward or express feelings or emotions. As we have seen, the eliciting of information about patient affect is widely regarded as a primary purpose of the therapeutic interaction. Whether an increase in the number of therapist communications about

TABLE 9

INCREASE IN SIMILARITY OF THE THERAPIST AND PATIENT BEHAVIOR OVER TIME

	Correlations between percentage of therapist and patient propositions		
	Sessions 1 and 2	*Sessions 5 and 6*	*2 Sessions from 3rd and 4th months*
Primary System	.72	.66	.88
Evaluation	.36	.45	.58
Affect	.23	.43	.70

n = 48 sessions (8 therapist-patient pairs)

affect results in an increased patient affective yield is a question of theoretical as well as practical interest.

In order to examine the possibility of an increase over time in the percentage of patient or therapist propositions defined in the above dimensions, we computed Pearson's coefficient of correlation (r) for three groups of sessions: sessions one and two; sessions five and six; and two sessions from the third and fourth months of therapy. Table 9 presents the correlations for the above three dimensions at three different times in therapy.

Table 9 shows that, for each dimension of communication, there is over time an increase in correlation, with an especially marked increase in the correlations for affective propositions.[4] These findings suggest that there is over time an increase in similarity of patient and therapist behavior with regard to these three areas.

One explanation for this increasing similarity of behavior is that it results from an increasing responsiveness of the patient and therapist toward each other's verbalizations. An increase in sensitivity would imply that if the patient discusses the process of therapy (primary system), the therapist is more likely to respond with propositions which are also about therapy. Similarly, if the therapist inquires of the patient as to how he felt about some event, the patient is more likely to respond with some proposition about his feelings. Our usage defines responsiveness simply as responding with the same subject or mode of communication.[5] How *degree* of responsiveness is measured is discussed later. We are here concerned with the process by which responsiveness is increased in therapy. This process can logically assume any of three different forms: (1) increasing responsiveness of the patient toward the therapist; (2) increasing responsiveness of the therapist toward the patient; or (3) increasing responsiveness of each toward the other.

Proceeding from one point of view it could be that the

tendency toward symmetry observed in our data is due to (1) an increased sensitivity on the part of the patient to the therapist's communications. From this vantage point, it is the therapist who extends positive sanctions for appropriate behavior (as exhibited by relevant verbal responses) and imposes negative sanctions for inappropriate behavior. It is the therapist who "knows" what the patient's role is, and it is the patient who must "learn" it by responding appropriately. However, it might be argued that increasing similarity is due to (2) an ever-increasing sensitivity of the therapist to the patient, as the therapist learns more about the patient. In this view, the therapist does not dominate the relationship, but is skilled in "following" wherever the patient leads. And finally, following through on the sociological generalization summarized by the Homans and Newcomb statements at the outset of this chapter, one would suspect that (3) both participants in a system contribute to the emergence of symmetry.

Since we have determined the correlations between therapist and patient propositions in eight actual therapies, we are in a position to specify which if any of the above hypotheses apply. In order to do this, we constructed an Index of Patient Responsiveness and an Index of Therapist Responsiveness.

The indices of responsiveness are based on comparing the character of a response (by the patient or by the therapist) with the character of the immediately preceding statement. Each index of responsiveness is defined as the ratio between the frequency of similar responses and the frequency of dissimilar responses. A ratio of 1.0 for the patient means that the patient responded in a similar manner *exactly as often* as he responded in a dissimilar manner. If the ratio were .5, it would mean that the patient responded in a similar manner only *one-half* as often as he responded in a dissimilar manner. Thus a ratio of 9.0 for the therapist means that the therapist responded in a similar manner 9 times as often as he responded in a dissimilar manner. For details on construction of this index, see note 6 at the end of this chapter.

Thus, if the Index of Therapist Responsiveness is higher in later phases of therapy than during the initial phases, it indicates that the therapist is becoming more sensitive to the patient's statements. In order to examine change over time, we grouped the sessions into four time periods: sessions one and two, sessions three through five, sessions six through eight, and two sessions taken from the third and fourth months of therapy. Then the Index of Patient Responsiveness and the Index of Therapist Responsiveness were computed for each time period for the three different dimensions of Primary System References, Evaluation, and Affect. The means for all eight patient-therapist pairs are reported in Tables 10, 11, and 12.

Table 10 shows that for Primary System References both the Index of Patient Responsiveness and the Index of Therapist Responsiveness increase strikingly from the earlier to later hours. Thus, in this case, the increased similarity of behavior seems to be due to the increased sensitivity of *both* the patient and the therapist to each other. However, it should be noted that the patient sensitivity increases at a more rapid rate than the therapist, and that the patient has a higher overall average responsiveness.

Table 11 shows that for Evaluative Propositions there is *no* increase either in the Index of Patient Responsiveness or in the Index of Therapist Responsiveness. Thus, in the case of evaluation, none of the above three hypotheses seems to apply, and the observed increase in correlations must be due to some other process. It is possible that there is a "delayed response" which escapes detection at this microscopic level of analysis. In other words, when the therapist gives an evaluative statement, the patient's evaluative response may be delayed for several interactions due to lack of immediate comprehension or the necessity for some thought before responding appropriately, etc. If

TABLE 10
PRIMARY SYSTEM RESPONSIVENESS OVER TIME

	Indices of primary system responsiveness				
	Sessions 1–2	*Sessions 3–5*	*Sessions 6–8*	*2 Sessions from 3rd and 4th months*	*All Sessions*
Patients	4.8	9.0	21.0	32.0	16.7
Therapists	5.9	9.4	8.1	11.5	8.7

n = 9,314 statements

TABLE 11
EVALUATIVE RESPONSIVENESS OVER TIME

	Indices of evaluative responsiveness				
	Sessions 1–2	*Sessions 3–5*	*Sessions 6–8*	*2 Sessions from 3rd and 4th months*	*All Sessions*
Patients	2.0	1.9	1.8	1.7	1.9
Therapists	1.4	1.2	1.3	1.2	1.3

n = 9,314 statements

TABLE 12
AFFECTIVE RESPONSIVENESS OVER TIME

	Indices of affective responsiveness				
	Sessions 1–2	*Sessions 3–5*	*Sessions 6–8*	*2 Sessions from 3rd and 4th months*	*All Sessions*
Patients	1.6	1.9	2.2	2.0	1.9
Therapists	1.7	1.9	1.9	1.9	1.9

n = 9,314 statements

this is the case, such a delayed sensitivity would not manifest itself in these indices since they reflect only the immediately following response. However, we may note that the averages show the patient to be on the whole more responsive than the therapist.

Turning now to our final category, Affective Propositions, Table 12 shows only a slight increase in the Index of Therapist Responsiveness and only a small increase in the Index of Patient Responsiveness. The increases in both therapist and patient affective responsiveness were so small that we might have overlooked a significant finding had we not examined each therapist separately. When we look at the indices computed separately for each therapist, we note two quite distinct patterns. The indices for therapist A and therapist B consistently increase over time, while the indices for therapist C and therapist D remain about the same or actually *decrease*. Thus it appears that the increased similarity of behavior of therapists A and B and their patients is due to increasing sensitivity of both the patients and therapists, while this is not true of therapists C and D, since neither they nor their patients show any consistent increase. A variety of measurements have shown that therapists A and B are more "active" than the other two. Perhaps active therapists "teach" their patients to become more sensitive to verbalization about affect. What might not have been expected was that the active therapists *themselves* would become more sensitive, while the more passive therapists did not. The question now remains, why is there an increasing correlation over time for the passive therapists as well as for the active therapists (see Table 9), even though no corresponding increase in responsiveness is measured by our index? Evidently, the increase in correlation must be due to a delayed rather than an immediate response.

Finally, one may ask why responsiveness differs both in magnitude and in rate of increase among these three dimensions.

In comparing responsiveness to primary system references with responsiveness to evaluative and affective propositions, we note a markedly higher responsiveness in the former than in the latter two dimensions. Not only is responsiveness to primary system reference initially high, but it increases at a faster rate for both patients and therapists. For example, the Index of Patient Responsiveness to primary system references in the later sessions shows that patients gave similar responses 32

TABLE 13

AFFECTIVE RESPONSIVENESS OVER TIME BY INDIVIDUAL THERAPIST

	Indices of Affective Responsiveness			
	Sessions 1–2	*Sessions 3–5*	*Sessions 6–8*	*2 Sessions from 3rd and 4th months*
Therapist A	1.2	1.8	1.9	3.1
Patients [a]	1.6	1.7	2.7	2.1
Therapist B	1.5	1.9	1.9	2.4
Patients	1.5	2.2	2.7	3.4
Therapist C	1.9	1.9	2.4	1.1
Patients	1.8	1.8	1.7	.7
Therapist D	2.2	2.1	1.5	.8
Patients	1.7	2.1	1.9	1.7

n = 80 sessions (9,314 statements)

[a] The Index of Patient Responsiveness used here represents the average score for the two patients of each therapist.

times as often as they gave dissimilar responses! This strikingly higher sensitivity may be related to the fact that primary system references are based on a specific substantive content, while the other two dimensions are based on characteristics of statements which are unrelated to the statements' specific content. In other words, a proposition coded as a primary system reference referred to concrete subject matter (therapy as a process).

On the other hand, a proposition which expressed opinion, wish, or preference was coded as Evaluative, regardless of subject matter under discussion. Similarly, a proposition which referred to any kind of feeling or emotion was coded as Affective, regardless of subject matter under discussion. Thus, the patient and therapist when communicating along the substantive dimension (Primary System Reference) were probably more aware of whether they were responding in a similar or dissimilar manner, than when communicating along the more abstract dimensions (evaluation and affect). This difference in awareness of degree of similarity in response may account for the striking difference in sensitivity.

A further factor which might have contributed to this extraordinary increase in Primary System Responsiveness (as contrasted with the smaller increase in Affective Responsiveness) may lie in the relative changes that occur in the frequency distributions of Primary System and Affective communications from the earlier to the later sessions. Primary system communications decrease considerably from the earlier to the later sessions, while verbalization about affect increases. It may therefore be the case that the occurrence of a Primary System communication in the later sessions is an especially significant signal.

SUMMARY

In this chapter we first correlated patient and therapist treatment sessions with respect to three dimensions of communicative acts (i.e. primary system references, evaluative and affective references). For example, the correlation coefficient for primary system references gave us a picture of the extent to which sessions high in therapist primary system references were also high in patient primary system references. We found that for each dimension there was an increase in the correlation between patient and therapist by session over time. The increase in the correlation for affective communication was especially marked.

There is then a growing similarity of patient and therapist behavior over time with respect to these three areas. Hypotheses were then formulated to account for this increase in similarity. Since the increase in similarity might be due to a change brought about by one or both of the participants, the data was analyzed to determine to which participant, patient or therapist, it could be attributed.

A participant may contribute to growing similarity of behavior during the session by responding with a proposition similar in kind to the one introduced by the other participant. The results suggested that for primary system communication, both therapist and patient are responsible for increased similarity. With regard to evaluative propositions, it was the patient who was more responsive throughout. There is, however, no increase in the responsiveness of either patient or therapist over time. With regard to affective references, two of the therapists (the two more active ones) and their patients show an increase in sensitivity.

A trend toward similarity is one type of interdependence noted between therapist and patient communications. It was to the specification of such phenomena that we referred, when we mentioned as our purpose the identification of latent social processes not within the awareness of the participants in a therapeutic system.

NOTES

1. Homans, *The Human Group,* p. 120.
2. Newcomb, "An Approach to the Study of Communicative Acts," *Psychological Review,* LX (1953), 393–404.
3. A method for such an analysis was tentatively formulated, but it could not be applied because a sponsor for this aspect of the research could not be found.
4. This finding is altogether to be expected, in the light of one of the well-known goals of analytic therapy, i.e., the freeing of the patient to express his feelings.
5. We do not mean to imply that responsiveness on the part of

the therapist is always "therapeutic" in the sense of responding to the patient's "needs." We are aware that responsiveness may also constitute therapist fulfillment of patient demands.

6. The Index of Patient Responsiveness is computed in three steps. The instructions which follow deal with the affective dimension, but they can be made applicable to any other dimension by replacing the term "affective" with the appropriate phrase.

(1) Calculate the proportion of therapist affective statements that are followed by patient affective statements. This is the proportion of similar affective responses.

(2) Calculate the proportion of therapist nonaffective statements which are followed by patient affective statements. This is the proportion of dissimilar responses.

(3) Divide the proportion of similar responses by the proportion of dissimilar responses. This gives an Index of Patient Responsiveness to affect. This Index is really a ratio of the frequency with which the patient responds in a similar manner to the frequency with which he responds in a dissimilar manner.

In order to illustrate this procedure, a simple example is worked through these three steps:

(1) Let us assume that for a certain group of sessions there are a total of 1000 therapist affective statements, 500 of which are followed by patient affective statements. This yields us a .50 similar response.

(2) In this same group of hours, there are also 1000 therapist nonaffective statements, 250 of which are followed by patient affective statements. This gives us a .25 dissimilar response.

(3) Dividing the proportion of similar responses (.50) by the proportion of dissimilar responses (.25) gives us a ratio of 2.0, which is the Index of Patient Responsiveness to Affect for the particular groups of hours. This index tells us that the patient responded in a similar manner twice as often as he responded in a dissimilar manner. If the ratio were 1.0, it would mean that the patient responded in a similar manner exactly as often as he responded in a dissimilar manner. If the ratio were .5, it would mean that the patient responded in a similar manner only one-half as often as he responded in a dissimilar manner.

The Index of Therapist Responsiveness is computed in the same way, except that the word "patient" is substituted for the word "therapist," and vice versa.

CHAPTER V

Equilibrium Processes

Section 1. Equilibrium within Sessions

We believe the concept of equilibrium to be as applicable to psychotherapy as it is to other interaction systems. The tendency of a system to maintain "a steady state" manifests itself in psychotherapy by the presence of limits within which certain system variables fluctuate. This is analogous to the limited range of variation found in blood sugar level and body temperature discussed earlier.

The work of Bales [1] as well as the earlier efforts of Chapple and Arensberg indicated that many types of groups exhibit in certain characteristics this limited range of variation.[2] For example, Chapple and Arensberg observed that two individuals working together in an industrial situation tend to arrive at a fairly stable interaction rate such that the interrelations between the amounts of activity contributed by two workers manifest a constant ratio. They found interaction rates to be a function both of the type of group involved and of the characteristics of the participants.

On this basis, we hypothesized at the outset of the study that for any given period of interaction the behavior emanating from the therapist and that emanating from the patient would tend to balance each other. For example, if the unit of analysis was quantity of speech, then the expectation was that the relative amounts of therapist and patient speech would stabilize at a fixed ratio and maintain that ratio during the course of the therapeutic interaction. When we examined this hypothesis for a communicational variable such as interaction rate—the pace at which therapist communications and patient communications follow upon one another (measured by averaging the number of interactions per transcribed page)—we find very little variation from session to session for any given therapist-patient pair. For example, the interaction rate ranges *among* different pairs from a high of 10 interactions per transcribed page for one patient-therapist pair to a low of 1.2 interactions per transcribed page for another therapist-patient pair. In contrast, however, the interaction rate for each therapist-patient pair varied very little from session to session. In four of our cases, the standard deviation in interaction rate from session to session was only 1.1. The highest standard deviation was 1.8.

The pace of interaction, therefore, appears to be fairly stable and varies very little over time for any given therapist-patient pair. A "steady" pace of interaction appears to be characteristic of a therapy system. There is a trend, shown by all pairs, toward stabilization at a lower interaction rate after the first or second month of therapy. This somewhat lower rate is then consistently reproduced session by session after that time. Each patient-therapist pair appears to establish an interaction rate "norm" from which it then varies very little.

We found the same equilibrium pattern when we looked at another variable, the ratio of therapist output to total output. Among the 120 coded sessions, we found a fairly broad range of therapist verbal output. Therapists contributed from as little as 3 percent to as much as 48 percent of the verbal output of a session. However, the average standard deviation was only 6.6 percent. This means that, in most sessions, the proportion of the total verbal output contributed by the therapist falls within 7 percent of the dyad's average therapist-patient output ratio.

This again suggests a tendency for the therapy system to maintain a steady state, this time in terms of the therapist's proportion of the output per session.

The limited variation in output which does occur need not be attributed entirely to the operation of random factors. We explored the hypothesis that this variation within given limits was due to another type of self-regulating process. This process concerns the maintenance of a fixed verbal output level for the session as a whole.

When we divided the sessions into two groups, those with more-than-average patient output and those with less-than-average patient output, we found an inverse relationship between patient and therapist output (as measured by the ratio of therapist to total output). That is, more than half (65 percent) of the sessions with above-average patient output show below-average therapist output, and more than half (61 percent) of the sessions with below-average patient output show above-average therapist output.[3] Thus, therapists compensate for higher patient output by reducing their own output and compensate for lower patient output by increasing their own output. This tends to make the total output for a given therapist-patient pair more constant and more stable than it would otherwise be.

Section 2. Equilibrium Processes from Session to Session

The search for equilibrium processes now moves from the level of the individual session to the level of sequences of sessions.

Each session as a part of the system of therapy is related to the preceding and succeeding session. We now wanted to ascertain whether disequilibrium or strain occurring within one session affected the structure of communication occurring within the subsequent session. In order to study such sequential compensating processes, it was first necessary to decide how to characterize sessions as to extent of strain present; to develop hypotheses as to what communicative acts could restore equilibrium in subsequent sessions; and then to examine our data.

As one indicator of session strain, we considered the number of silences per session. A large number of silences in a session may reflect a breakdown of communication, or a "resistance." During some silences, productive "internal communication" or reverie takes place, but it seemed likely that sessions containing 10 or 20 extended silences were sessions in which verbalization was impaired (a pause was not counted as a silence unless it was over 10 seconds in length).

We classified 66 sessions, for which every immediately following session had also been coded, into high-, middle-, and low-silence sessions. We then examined the structure of communication in the session immediately following each session which had been classified. We found that the sessions exhibiting most silences were succeeded by sessions characterized by a higher percentage of therapist evaluative acts and therapist acts of high informational specificity. In fact, for each pair, the sessions with the most silences were followed by sessions with a higher average percentage of therapist evaluation than those with the least silences. The finding is reported in Table 14.

A similar finding with respect to informational specificity applies to sessions following those with a high number of silences. On the average, each session following upon a high-silence session exhibits more therapist informational specificity than does a session following one with a low number of silences. In the sessions following those with a high number of silences, 66 percent of the therapist's verbal output falls into the four categories highest in informational specificity (categories 5, 6, 7, 8), while for sessions following a low number of silences only 56 percent of the therapist's verbal output falls into these categories. Thus, a movement in the direction of informational specificity is part of the therapist's response to silence in the preceding session.

The number of questions was another indicator of session strain. We hypothesized that a large number of questions reflected a certain amount of misunderstanding and confusion with respect to patient-therapist role expectations, i.e., discrepancy between patient and therapist conceptions. Therapist questions such as "Why do you supose you feel this way?" represent therapist efforts to cope with this discrepancy.

TABLE 14
THERAPIST EVALUATIVE PROPOSITIONS IN SESSIONS FOLLOWING HIGH- AND LOW-SILENCE SESSIONS

	Proportion of therapist evaluative propositions in the next session							
Number of silences in session	*Therapist A*	*Therapist B*		*Therapist C*		*Therapist D*		*All Therapists*
	Patient 1	*Patient 1*	*Patient 2*	*Patient 1*	*Patient 2*	*Patient 1*	*Patient 2*	
High	.19	.52	.38	.24	.19	.25	.34	.29
Low	.18	.40	.28	.09	.14	.12	.31	.22

n = 64 sessions

Comparing the proportion of therapist evaluative and informationally specific propositions in sessions subsequent to sessions with a large number of therapist questions with those subsequent to sessions low in questions, we found differences not as great as discussed above, but still in the expected direction. Three of the four therapists took account of the strain reflected in a large number of questions by increasing evaluation and informational specificity in the following session. It appears to us that the increase in evaluative statements could be directly attributed to the presence of a large number of questions in the previous sessions. Evaluations (i.e., interpretations) in subsequent sessions may thus refer to the material obtained by therapist inquiries in previous sessions.

Still another indicator of system strain was assumed to be low therapist volume of verbal output. We found evidence, presented elsewhere in this book, that low therapist output was associated with patient dissatisfaction with communication. Three measures of therapist volume were used in the development of an index (1) the number of therapist propositions per session, (2) the ratio of therapist output to total output, and (3) the average number of exchanges per page. These three measures were combined into a single index of therapist output. Sessions were first ranked for each of the three indicators separately and then a single rank for each session was determined by averaging the three measures. Sessions were then grouped into three groups of sessions, ranking high, middle, and low in therapist volume. Three of the four therapists increased primary system (patient-therapist role) discussions in the sessions following upon those with low volume. Over 50 percent more primary system discussions follow sessions with low therapist volume than follow those with high volume (13 percent vs. 8 percent).

At this point, it should be noted that the mechanisms involved are not conceived of in some purely formal and mechanistic sense. Although we do not undertake to do so here, we believe it to be possible to account for these phenomena on a content or therapy-oriented level. For example, consider the above-mentioned relationship between low therapist output in a session and the subsequent increase in therapist primary system communication. It is precisely the lack of verbal contribution in the preceding session upon which the patient comments in the subsequent session and which prompts the therapist into an exploration of the roles of patient and therapist, the division of responsibility involved, etc. (communication which is classified as primary system communication).

Equilibrium processes in psychotherapy can also be seen in the marked pattern of oscillation shown from session to session in the proportion of therapist output for each session. We illustrate this in Fig. 8. Figure 8 shows that when the proportion of the therapist output in each of two pairs is plotted over time for consecutive sessions, there is a striking tendency for the proportion of the output to oscillate around the mean. If the proportion for one session is below the mean, then—with some exceptions—the proportion for the second session is above the mean, and the proportion for the third session is below the mean, and so on. It is almost as if there were some kind of accounting system that compensated for lower therapist output in one hour by eliciting a higher therapist output in the following hour. Or, to use another analogy, it is as if proportion of output acted like a pendulum which must swing back in the other direction with each successive session.

In contrast to this oscillating pattern, Fig. 9 presents a pattern describing constant proportion of therapist output over time.

Both patterns represent some kind of equilibrium process. The therapist who maintains a constant proportion of output from session to session must establish a constant ratio between his output and that of his patient so that when his patient is more active, he becomes more active, and vice versa. Thus, he maintains an equilibrium with respect to ratio of output.

The therapist who varies his ratio of output is more difficult to account for. His activity level is not a function of the patient's activity within the sessions. Instead, it appears to be a function of the therapist's own activity level in the preceding session. In this case also, therapist output seems to show a systematic variation over time.

Section 3. Equilibrium Processes over the Life of the System

Having examined equilibrium processes as they occur *within* sessions and those that occur *between* sessions, we shall now

FIGURE 8
EXAMPLES OF OSCILLATING RATIO OF THERAPIST OUTPUT TO TOTAL OUTPUT OVER TIME

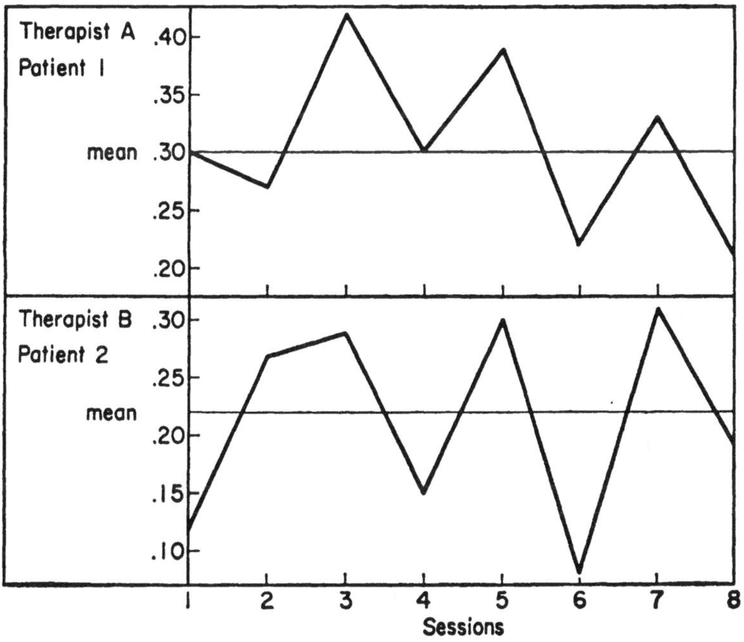

FIGURE 9
AN EXAMPLE OF CONSTANT RATIO OF THERAPIST OUTPUT TO TOTAL OUTPUT OVER TIME

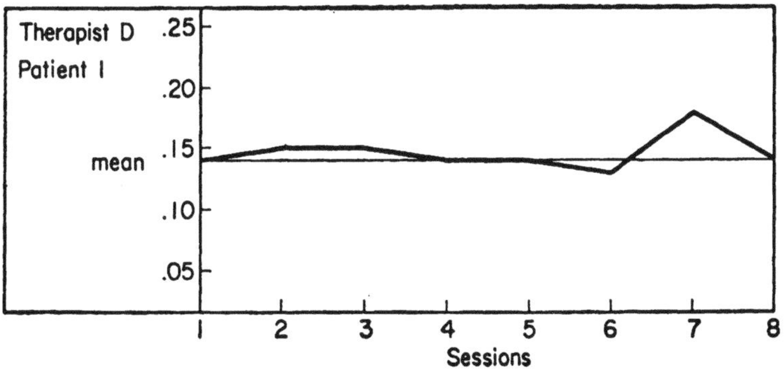

examine equilibria as they are manifested by the system as a whole.

Like any other action system, therapist-patient systems seem to exhibit self-regulating and self-maintaining tendencies that establish equilibria at various levels and set limits within which variation is stabilized. Anything that tends to disequilibrate the system calls forth compensatory processes within the system that move the system variables back in the direction of equilibrium.

INDICATIONS OF STRAIN IN THE THERAPY SYSTEM AS A WHOLE

When the system is in a state of disequilibrium, it manifests signs of system "strain," and the adjustments that take place within the system are toward the elimination of such strain. The processes we now have in mind relate to the very existence of the therapy system itself, not to strains within any particular subsystem or unit of therapy. We will now explore several indicators of system strain (disequilibrium) in psychotherapy systems.

1. *Discontinuance of treatment.* Obviously the most extreme indication of system malfunction due to excessive system strain and disequilibrium is the disintegration of the system itself. A premature termination of treatment may be taken as a sign that there was some sort of failure on the part of system homeostasis such that the internal stabilizing and re-equilibrating mechanisms failed to preserve the system. Of course, when the treatment system has achieved its goals, termination of treatment is a natural and desirable consequence. This is a "natural death" of a system that has performed its function. On the other hand, perpetuation of the system does not necessarily mean that therapeutic goals are being accomplished. Sometimes, as we know, relationships are maintained only because some of the "goals" have been abandoned by the participants.

It cannot be claimed that the maintenance of the therapist-patient relationship and the accomplishment of therapy are always synonomous.

Three of our patients did in fact terminate "prematurely,"[4] but eight remained in treatment for the duration of the research (eight months). Of these latter eight patients, five discontinued when the end of the project terminated their special fee status.

2. *Broken Appointments.* Another indicator taken to be a sign of system strain is the number of broken appointments. A broken appointment was defined as a psychotherapy session whose time and place were agreed upon by the patient and therapist but which was cancelled by the patient less than 24 hours in advance, or was simply not attended by the patient. Some of the "reasons" given by the patients for broken appointments were: patient forgot the appointment; patient got a headache, upset stomach, or other illness shortly before the appointment time; patient fell asleep on the bus or subway on the way to the appointment and did not wake up until it was too late; and patient set up a conflicting appointment, such as dinner with friends or a theater party shortly before the psychotherapy appointment. Any or all of these "reasons" could easily be rationalizations to avoid attending the psychotherapy session. It is widely claimed by psychotherapists that appointments broken by a patient for excuses such as those above are manifestations of patient resistance or unconscious desire to avoid the psychotherapy session.[5] We considered such resistance as symptomatic of system strain. The use of broken appointments as an indicator of system strain is analogous to the use of absentee rates in business and factories as an indicator of morale.[6] Lack of morale should be closely related to system strain.

3. *Patients' verbalizations.* Other indications of system strain can be observed in the verbatim transcripts, but they are not

easily quantified. These are patient outbursts overtly expressing dissatisfaction with the therapy interaction. In these, the patient actually verbalizes his perception and experience of strain in the therapeutic relationship. Many of his complaints are directed against the therapist's lack of activity. It appears that the patient is complaining because the therapist has not taken the action necessary to relieve the system of strain so that the patient can feel more comfortable. A certain amount of patient dissatisfaction, frustration, and tension is considered—in analytic theory—both a necessary and a basic part of psychotherapy. Patient expectations derived from other settings (i.e., transference) cannot be met in the therapeutic setting. In fact, these expectations and their frustration form one of the basic subject matters of therapy. Yet as Menninger states: "Obviously the mounting sense of deprivation and frustration cannot go on indefinitely . . . . the desired effect can be obtained only if the frustration tension is held within a certain optimum range." [7]

Some examples of patient verbalizations about system strain are offered here for illustrative purposes:

Patient: Well, I feel, uh, it would be a little frustrating for me if I didn't receive some sort of an interpretation, some sort of feeling anyway.

Patient: They (psychiatrists) wait for you to say something, and uh, just sit around and look at you, completely devoid of any expression at all, no comments, nothing, and just wait. Well, now I've come to you for one reason, that is to get help. I'm not coming for any other reason. If it weren't for that, I would never meet you, or have occasion to meet you.

Therapist: Um.

Patient: And this is something that just, I just knot up inside. And, uh, I don't think its anything strictly with me, because I've talked to other people and I've had, uh treatment or visits, or whatever you call it, and they say that this is something more or less routine, this is what psychiatrists do, this way of sitting. And well, it creates a horrible feeling inside me, when I feel like a fool too,

I have to fight to think up things to say, and I get this antagonistic feeling toward you. And I think it's detrimental to my being able to open up.

Patient: I wish you would ask me some questions because I just can't do. Pulling these things out, they feel so disjointed and disconnected, I just wonder if I'll ever get anyplace.

We intend to show in the following paragraphs that certain forms of activity on the part of the therapist reduce the amount of strain manifested by the therapy system. We are then going to try to identify the precise nature of such activities and to offer some hypotheses explaining why they have the effect of restoring equilibrium to the system. Since we do not have satisfactory operational definitions as to when a patient's experience of strain is "optimal" and when it is "excessive," we are limiting ourselves to a comparison between those of our therapeutic dyads that show *less* strain and those that show *more* strain, as measured by the three indicators described above. We do not take a position with respect to whether strain is a "desirable" or an "undesirable" condition of a therapy system. We merely describe some of the activities that reduce strain (as measured by the three indicators) when it is manifest.

Further, we are very well aware that therapists differ in their convictions as to how much deprivation is therapeutic, and that inactivity is theoretically justified—in analytic theory—on a number of grounds: (1) inactivity on the part of the therapist highlights and reflects back to the patient a consciousness of his own defenses and resistances; (2) the goal of free association is interfered with by therapist activity; (3) the therapist should not be too responsive to the patient's excessive dependency; and (4) therapist activity prevents the patient from revealing his own personal feelings, preferences, values, etc.

In Table 15 we show our findings for the four therapists paired in terms of "activeness," therapists A and B being more active than therapists C and D. They are more active with respect to (1) rate of interaction (the average number of exchanges per transcribed page); (2) volume of verbal output (average number of propositions per session); (3) relative verbal output (proportion of total output of the session contributed by them); (4) subject changes (the average number of times the therapist changes the subject per session); (5) primary system references (average number of therapist propositions per session that refer to primary system); (6) evaluation and prescription (proportion of therapist propositions that are evaluative-prescriptive); and (7) informational specificity (proportion of therapists' propositions that are informationally highly specific).[8]

Table 15 also shows that with respect to the three criteria of system strain (discontinuance of treatment, broken appointments, and patient complaints), the dyads in which the therapists were more active show the least signs of strain.

The significance of the terminations is somewhat obscured by practical and methodological difficulties. When the period of time for which the therapists had agreed to carry the patients at reduced fees (eight months) had elapsed, the therapists gave their patients the option of continuing in treatment at their regular fee. Our data show (see Table 15, item 9) that three out of the four patients of the more active therapists elected to remain in treatment, while the four patients of the less active therapists for a variety of reasons had to discontinue. We cannot be certain of all the factors contributing to this finding, and it should not by itself be given too much weight.

However, broken appointments (see Table 15, item 10) also occurred less frequently in the dyads of the more active therapists. During the first 25 sessions of therapy, we found no broken appointments among the patients of our two more active therapists, while a total of ten broken appointments occurred among the patients of the two less active therapists, each of their patients having broken at least one appointment.

TABLE 15
THERAPIST ACTIVITIES AND INDICATIONS OF SYSTEM STRAIN

Description of indicators	*More active therapists*		*Less active therapists*	
	Therapist A	*Therapist B*	*Therapist C*	*Therapist D*
ACTIVENESS				
1. Rate of interaction	7.0	5.2	4.0	3.2
2. Propositional output per session	142	106	58	48
3. Proportion of total verbal output of session	.45	.29	.17	.16
4. Number of subject changes per session	12.0	6.2	6.2	4.3
5. Number of primary System propositions per session	48	24	14	13
6. Proportion of propositions that are evaluative-prescriptive	.32	.46	.18	.29
7. Proportion of propositions with high informational specificity	.47	.44	.24	.32
8. Proportion of propositions with low informational specificity	.15	.04	.26	.27
SYSTEM STRAIN				
9. Number of patients who discontinue treatment after completion of research	1	0	2	2
10. Number of broken appointments during first 25 sessions	none	none	3	7
11. Patients' complaints about system strain	few	few	many	many

Thus, insofar as a broken appointment may be conceded to be a sign of strain within therapy systems, the systems within which there was less activity manifested the most strain.

Clear "expressions of situational dissatisfaction" occurred frequently in the transcripts of the less active therapists. All of the verbatim materials used earlier to illustrate this form of dissatisfaction are from the transcripts of the less active therapists. One reason why expressions of situational dissatisfaction occurred so infrequently in the transcripts of the more active therapists is that these therapists *did* respond to their patients' felt need for verbal feedback and thus reduced the system strain. Still, the occurrence of such remarks is interpreted as evidence of greater strain in the dyads of the less active therapists.

We have attempted to show that the maintenance of equilibrium and the reduction of system strain (as measured by our indicators) is associated with therapist activeness. We shall now attempt to determine through what means activeness on the part of the therapist brings about this reduction in strain and restoration of equilibrium.

SYSTEM MAINTENANCE THROUGH THERAPIST ACTIVENESS

We shall see in Chapter X that patients report more satisfaction (less strain) for sessions in which therapists have been verbally more active. Sheer verbal activity per se (within limits) provides the patient with more reinforcement, feedback, and information. Moreover, the findings reported in Table 15 show that the two therapists who are verbally more active in a quantitative sense (higher interaction rate, greater volume of output, and higher proportion of total output) are also more active in a qualitative sense (more change of subject, more informationally specific, evaluative-prescriptive, and primary system references). Thus they feed into the system more of the activities that tend to stabilize and re-equilibrate it.

Informational Specificity as an Equilibrium-Maintaining Mechanism. Propositions that are informationally more active, i.e., that contain a greater quantity of information in the sense of informational specificity, are used by the active therapists to maintain the greater amount of equilibrium found in their dyads. Low-specificity statements are more ambiguous than high-specificity statements, and our findings support the findings of Bordin [9] that low informational specificity (ambiguity) tends to increase patient anxiety ("strain"). Or, to put it more affirmatively, high informational specificity reduces anxiety.

We have already suggested that frequency of patient silences may be used as a rough indication of communicational strain. In our data, we found that silences followed 19 percent of therapist statements that were low in informational specificity but that the use of statements of high informational specificity reduced this percentage to 15 percent.

High informational specificity on the part of therapists increases cognitive clarity and hence the amount of information the patient receives about *what* the therapist is talking about. In Sullivan's words, it provides "consensual validation." When a therapist uses a low-specificity statement, the patient is less sure about what is expected of him and this tends to increase his situational dissatisfaction and sense of strain.[10]

Attempts on the part of the patient to reduce strain and reestablish expectational equilibrium should lead him to search for material to which the therapist may respond more positively. Thus frequent changes in subject matter on the part of patients may be considered to be a sign of uncertainty on the patient's part or a sign of a difference in expectations between patient and therapist. Our data show that 32 percent of therapist low-specificity statements are followed by a change of subject on the part of the patient. This percentage is halved (i.e., it is reduced to 17 percent) by therapist use of high specificity statements.

We have shown that these reductions in the amount of patient silence and in the number of subject changes by the patient are accomplished through the use of statements that are high in informational specificity. This finding supports the hypothesis that informational specificity reduces strain and maintains equilibrium. The system strain is reduced because information is fed into the system at a time when the system is out of balance because of lack of adequate communication between the therapist and his patient. By clarifying and eliminating disequilibria due to lack of information, the informationally specific statement restores the system to its "normal" state.

It should be noted that the findings reported here are based on data from all four therapists. The less active therapists too will sometimes employ "activeness" to maintain equilibrium.

Primary System Reference as an Equilibrium Maintaining Mechanism. Primary system references are propositions in which the therapist and patient discuss problems relating to what therapy is all about. We discuss elsewhere the importance of role learning in psychotherapy. The patient has to learn a new set of expectations appropriate to his function as a patient in the therapeutic relationship. When a patient's initial expectations are not met, he experiences disappointment or frustration. Dissimilarity in expectations itself is a form of disequilibrium.

If the patient expects to make rapid progress within a few sessions and does not learn that this expectation is unrealistic, he may become so discouraged that he will terminate treatment when the expected progress does not materialize. If he expects the therapist to be a parent figure toward him (telling him exactly what to do, loving and reprimanding him), he may terminate treatment when the disappointment reaction sets in, or he may enter a stage of resistance until his misconceptions are exposed and corrected. If a patient expects to tell the therapist only those things of which he is proud and hides those things of which he is ashamed, the patient will make little progress until he learns to do otherwise. Thus, unrealistic role expectations tend to increase system strain and to destroy equilibrium.

Primary system references center around role discussion. The more primary system references on the part of the patient, the more information the patient is soliciting about his role in treatment. The more primary system references on the part of the therapist, the more the therapist is teaching the patient his proper role in therapy. Primary system references therefore reduce strain and disequilibrium by clarifying role expectations and reducing the lack of complimentarity between the patient's and the therapist's conceptions of therapy.

This hypothesis is supported by item 5 of Table 15, which shows that the dyads exhibiting the least strain are also those in which primary system references by the therapists are the most frequent.

This role teaching seems to pay off in terms of patient learning. Figure 10 is a graph showing the average number of primary system propositions spoken per session by the two more active therapists (solid line), by the two more passive therapists (dash-dot line), by the patients of the more active therapists (dash line), and by the patients of the more passive therapists (dotted line), through four time periods. The first three sessions comprise the first time period, the next three sessions comprise the second time period, sessions seven and eight comprise the third time period, and the final time period is made up of a sample for each dyad of three sessions taken from the third and fourth months of therapy. There are three important contrasts to be noted in Fig. 10. First, we see that the active therapists allot many more propositions during the early sessions to discussion of therapist-patient roles than do the passive therapists. Secondly, while the active therapists produce *more* primary system propositions than do their patients, the passive therapists produce *less* primary system propositions than their patients. This appears to mean that the active therapists take the lead in discussing therapist-patient roles while passive therapists seem to avoid role discussion even when their patients introduce it. Thirdly, we see that for the dyads in which there is an active therapist, the amount of role teaching that occurs is initially large but diminishes rapidly, becoming very low in the last time period; while for dyads in which there is a passive therapist, the amount of role discussion

FIGURE 10

MEAN NUMBER OF PRIMARY SYSTEM PROPOSITIONS PER SESSION FOR ACTIVE AND PASSIVE THERAPISTS AND THEIR PATIENTS OVER TIME

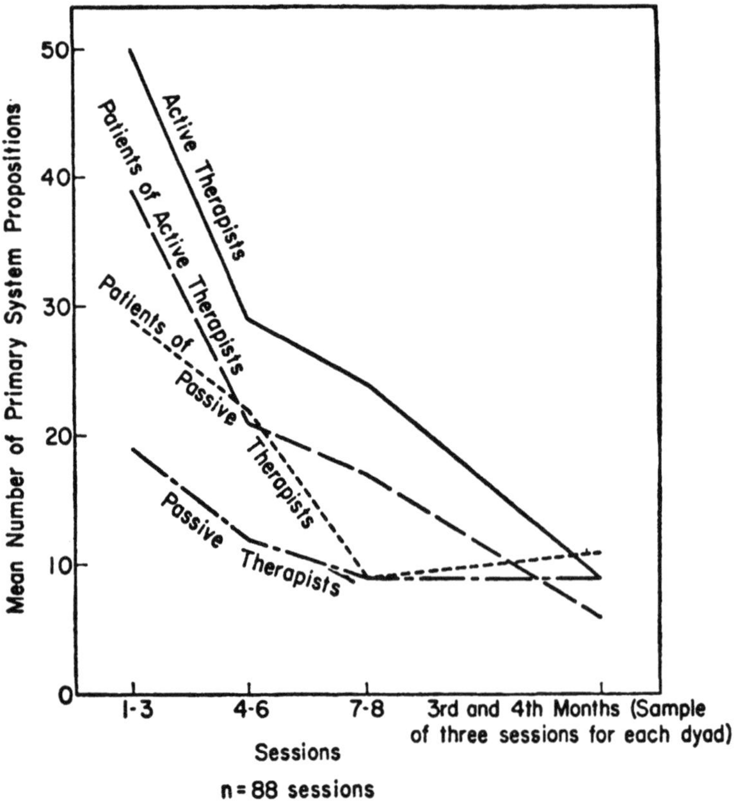

remains about the same from the third to the fourth time period.

Of special interest are the curves of the patients. It can be seen in Fig. 10 that the amount of role discussion engaged in by the patients of the active therapists is initially much higher than the amount of role discussion engaged in by the patients of the passive therapists. By the fourth month of treatment, however, the situation is reversed. At that time, the patients of the passive therapists are engaged in about twice as much primary role system discussion as the patients of the active therapists.

In Chapter IX we will present data to show that primary system information is used by both active and passive therapists to achieve equilibrium when the system of expectations is in a state of disequilibrium (expectational dissimilarity).

Evaluation and Prescription as an Equilibrium-Maintaining Mechanism. It will be recalled that evaluative propositions "express or ask for appraisals, opinions, or statements of value," and that prescriptive propositions "express or ask for imperatives or directives." Parsons has drawn attention to what he calls the "manipulation of rewards system." In psychotherapy, the reward system though fairly subtle is nonetheless real and important to the patients. Rewards range all the way from explicit statements of approval by the therapist to a nod of agreement or a mere grunt of interest or even a raised eyebrow. Studies [11] have shown that, in interview situations, grunts of interest and other such minimal stimuli serve as powerful rewards or "reinforcers." Punishments range all the way from explicit statements of disapproval to a slight frown or simply a lack of response, which the patient can interpret either as lack of interest or as disapproval. Below are two examples of patient requests for some kind of evaluation and therapist avoidance of giving it:

Patient: (*clearing throat*) Do you think we're getting anywhere, Doctor?

Therapist: What do you think?

Patient: First of all, today, I'd like to ask, uh, if you have any criticism to make of myself as a patient. Is, uh, is there anything wrong with my, uh, attitude, conscious or unconscious that I can possibly do something about. Uh, is, uh, has anything I said wasted any time as far as you know, uh, or have I been trying to get at the right thing so far?

Therapist: Well, uh, may I ask you how do you feel about this?

Patient: (*laughs*) That's what I expected.

By contrast, here are some examples of manipulation of rewards by the therapist:

Patient: I'm not being a very good patient, am I?

Therapist: Well, I think you are a very fine patient. What makes you think that you're not?

Patient: Well, I'm not talking at all.

Therapist: You're talking *very* well.

Patient: . . . They're all very friendly, they think I'm very nice, smart, but, uh. I'm just nice, that's all, there's nothing to me. I'm just a nice fellow.

Therapist: (*laugh*) That's *something*. What makes you feel that being nice isn't quite an achievement?

Patient: Well, in a sense you're right, that all you did do was make that observation, and it was a correct observation. On the other hand, I think that I have some right in what I'm saying in that, uh, well, I said what I mean to say again, when somebody makes a—

Therapist: Why are you so cautious?

Patient: Am I being cautious?

Therapist: Very cautious . . .

Patient: I was going to say I don't always lie down and whine at misfortune, sometimes I fight back.

Therapist: Well, that's fine.

Fundamental to contemporary learning theory is the concept of reinforcement (manipulation of rewards). Production of differentiation (both of stimulus and of response) was demonstrated as early as the time of Pavlov's work to be a function of differential manipulation of reinforcement. Every proposition or signal (even silences) emanating from a therapist acts as either negative or positive reinforcement (sanction) for the patient, and so there is no question as to *whether* a psychotherapist manipulates a reward system in psychotherapy.[12] The only question is how often, how consciously, and how systematically he utilizes it to acomplish the goals of therapy. That the *amount* of reward manipulation is greater in the dyads of the more active therapists goes almost without saying, for by definition the more active therapists are more active because they produce more propositions and hence more communicational acts in every activity category (see Table 15). We can also see (Table 15, item 6) that the proportion of the therapist output devoted to evaluation and prescription is almost twice as great for the more active therapists. The actual number of communicational acts in every activity category is also greater, since the active therapists produce a greater total number of propositions. Since all statements containing expressions of approval or disapproval fall into these categories, we see that the more active therapists not only administer a greater amount of reinforcement in general, but also that they devote a larger proportion of their output to the categories of appraisal, opinion, and values. Since the more active therapists engage in a great deal more reinforcing activity than the less active therapists, we may now ask the more general question of how reinforcement is related to system equilibrium.

Reinforcement leads to conditioning or learning. We assume in accordance with classical learning concepts that greater reinforcement in the form of primary system references leads to greater learning about the conditions and procedures of treatment. This greater learning shows up not only in the more rapid drop in the propositions devoted to this topic, but also in the replies to questions about topics upon which the patients most wished clarification. The fact that later on in therapy the patients of the less active therapists still asked for clarification about the primary system is taken by us to be a sign of disequilibrium. Zeigarnik[13] demonstrated that incomplete tasks tend toward completion (equilibrium). In this sense, one can consider an unacknowledged communication of the patient as an incomplete task demanding completion. By their communicational activeness, the more active therapists tend to fulfill or satisfy many more of their patients' communicational requests than do the less active therapists, and in this manner they reduce the amount of disequilibrium in their dyads. Learning, then, not only creates disequilibrium by creating new requests and new questions, but it can also serve the function of reestablishing equilibrium by satisfying requests and answering questions.

Let us now address ourselves to the specific role that evaluative-prescriptive propositions play in the reinforcement picture. We suggest that the therapists reinforce and extinguish patient responses by means of their reinforcement patterns. By virtue of his greater activity, the more active therapist administers a greater amount of reinforcement than does the less active therapist. We also assume that, because there is more reinforcement, there is more learning. More learning is not necessarily better learning, and we do not contend that what is learned is necessarily therapeutic. We are merely taking note of the fact that the greater activity of the active therapists produces greater changes in their patients' verbal behavior than occur in the patients of the less active therapists.

The more active therapists devote a greater proportion, almost half, of their activities to evaluative and prescriptive statements. Another way of putting this is that the less active therapists not only engage in less reinforcement activities in general, but also actually seem to avoid using evaluative and prescriptive propositions. In a sense, they seem consciously to avoid manipulation of the reward system. They seem determined to permit the patient to learn for himself. The patient must thus proceed in therapy with a minimum of direction from the therapist. On the other hand, the more active therapist is constantly structuring the situation for the patient. He not only reinforces this and that, but he consciously appraises and evaluates and prescribes. We suspect that one can go too far in either direction.

SUMMARY

The tendency of the therapy system to maintain "a steady state" manifests itself by the presence of limits within which certain system variables fluctuate. For any given period (e.g., within a session, between two sessions, and over the first eight months of therapy), the behaviors of the therapist and of the patient tend to counterbalance each other.

Each therapist-patient pair establishes by the second month of therapy an interaction rate "norm" from which it then varies very little. This also appears to be true of the ratio of therapist to patient verbal output. For most sessions, the proportion of the total output contributed by the therapist falls within 7 percent of the dyad's average therapist-patient output ratio. Therapists compensate for higher patient output by reducing their own output and compensate for lower patient output by increasing their output. This tends to stabilize the total output of the session.

Sessions that tend to disequilibrate the system as a whole are followed by sessions containing compensating processes that tend to restore the system to within its "normal" limits. The "system-oriented" therapists maintain equilibrium by a remarkably clear pattern of oscillation from session to session around their own mean proportion of output. In this case, output rises above their mean in one session and falls below the mean in the next. In contrast to this oscillating pattern, the "theory oriented" therapists maintain equilibrium by establishing a constant proportion of output from session to session from which they vary very little.

Signs such as discontinuance of treatment, broken appointments, and verbalizations of situational dissatisfaction by the patients signal disturbances (disequilibrium) in the functioning of the therapy system as a whole. Increased activeness, greater informational specificity, more primary system information, more evaluation and more prescription comprise the means employed by therapists to minimize strain and maintain equilibrium in the system as a whole.

NOTES

1. Bales, "In Conference," *Harvard Business Review*, XXXII (March–April, 1954), 44–51.
2. Chapple and Arensberg, "Measuring Human Relations," *Genetic Psychology Monograph*, XXII (1940), 3–147.
3. This relationship is significant at the .01 level.
4. One patient terminated after the third session because he considered that he had made sufficient progress to cut down his visits to once every two weeks. This was not acceptable to the therapist. For the other two patients, faulty recordings of the first two sessions (which we felt were critical for the research) and the feeling on the part of the therapist that the cases were not quite suitable for analytic psychotherapy led to termination.
5. For example, see Wolberg, *The Technique of Psychotherapy*, pp. 346, 465, 471, 514.
6. For example, see Katz and Hyman, "Industrial Morale and Public Opinion Methods," *International Journal of Opinion and Attitude Research*, Vol. I, No. 3, pp. 13–30.
7. Menninger, *Theory of Psychoanalytic Technique*, p. 57.
8. For the purpose of this analysis, propositions were scored as low in informational specificity if they fell into the lowest three categories of informational specificity, and were scored as high in informational specificity if they fell into the highest three categories. In informational categories (1) and (2), the therapist merely encourages the patient to talk without limiting him to anything specific. In Category (3), the therapist is slightly more specific because he refers to a general subject matter area. In Category (8) the therapist specifically excludes discussion, in Category (7) he limits the patient to a specific reply, and in Category (6) he interprets.

We regard the latter three categories of communication as representing qualitatively more activity than the former three categories, since they are more controlling.

9. Bordin, "Ambiguity as a Therapeutic Variable," *Journal of Consulting Psychology,* LXX (1955), 1–15.

10. In analytic treatment, the analyst may consciously employ low-specificity statements for the purpose of generating a certain amount of patient dissatisfaction, a condition which the therapist regards as a desirable therapeutic objective.

11. For example, see Salzinger and Pisoni, "Reinforcement of Affect Responses of Schizophrenics during the Clinical Interview," paper read at the Eastern Psychological Association Meeting, 1957; or see Greenspoon, "The Reinforcing Effect of Two Spoken Sounds on the Frequency of Two Responses," *American Journal of Psychology,* LXVIII (1956), 409–416.

12. Reid, "The Problem of Values in Psychoanalysis," *American Journal of Psychoanalysis,* XV (1955 No. 2), 119–120.

> . . . it remains undeniable that in a hundred ways, both gross and subtle, the analyst will inevitably show his moral colors and what side he takes on many a controversial issue about the rights and wrongs, the goods and evils, in some problematic area under analysis. . . . For here, as elsewhere, actions—and inactions are of course kinds of actions—often speak louder than words and sometimes less ambiguously, while the inexplicit meanings of casually expressed interventions frequently carry more weight, particularly in the mind of a patient with a hyperactive superego who is always morally on guard, than would explicitly formulated moral judgements.

13. Zeigarnik, "Uber das Behalten von Erledigten und Unerledigten Handlungen," *Psychologische Forschungen,* IX (1927), 1–86.

Part Three

THERAPY AS AN INFORMATIONAL EXCHANGE SYSTEM

CHAPTER VI

Informational Structure in Psychotherapy

Terms such as communication and information are being used more and more in the discussion of the therapeutic relationship. According to Ruesch, this current shift away from describing the therapist-patient interaction purely in the vocabulary of psychoanalysis is accounted for by the circumstance that "no appropriate concepts or language exist which enable doctors to be aware of or talk about *second by second changes* which occur in the course of therapy. The conceptual schemes available and the language actually spoken by therapists signify primarily long term, almost secular changes in the personality of the patients . . . the psychotherapist in his daily and momentary reactions is *message* oriented and only in his overall attitude is he patient oriented. Any principle, attitude or goal of his can be implemented only through an *actual communicative exchange*" (italics added).[1]

Patients convey information about their dreams, their sex life, their feelings about the therapist, etc. While the primacy of information transmission in the performance of the patient role in therapy is easily seen, equal recognition has not been accorded to the informational character of the therapist role. As Harry Stack Sullivan wrote, "The situation is never so simply one-sided. It is never one who gives and one who takes. While it may be hard to see in some cases, there is always a measure of exchange of information." [2] One advantage of conceiving of the therapeutic interaction in terms of information flow is that it thus can more readily be quantified and systematically studied.

Sullivan states that "The principal problem of the therapeutic interview is that of facilitating the accession to awareness of information which will clarify for the patient the more troublesome aspects of his life." This awareness of information is gained through communication. ". . . one has information about one's experiences only to the extent that one has tended to communicate it to another—or thought about it in the manner of communicative speech." [3]

From this point of view, a major objective of psychotherapy is to maximize the quantity of information available to the patient. The assumption underlying this goal of treatment is that as more information becomes available to the patient about his feelings, his relationships, his past, his current objectives, etc., his understanding and his ability to act more effectively increase. It is worth noting parenthetically that the psychoanalytic formulation of "making the unconscious, conscious" is another way of describing the process of making available (conscious) to the patient information which is not presently accessible (unconscious) to him. Seen in this light, the therapist's job in treatment is to increase the quantity of information available to his patient. Thus his informational role in therapy differs considerably from that of his patient. The patient's role requires him to supply information about himself. But the therapist's role requires him to supply information of a different sort. Instead of providing information about himself, the therapist provides the patient with verbal stimuli containing information that may help the patient to increase his own knowledge about himself and the world around him.

The patient presents the doctor with a fact—let us say a complaint; the therapist is given thereby a partial orientation and is enabled to ask a more pointed question of the patient. This directs the patient's attention and thinking toward further self-exploration, the communication of which to the therapist in turn enables the latter to make a comment. This comment throws a new light on something from the patient and enables him to add further material which then still further enlightens the physician who may then still further assist the patient objectively to appraise himself and so on.[4]

Clearly what the therapist says or does not say will have an influence upon what the patient is likely to say or not say. So long as the patient is responsive, verbal stimuli from the therapist are among the factors that determine what he will talk about. The more limiting, focusing, or directive the therapist's comments are, the more they will tend to control the patient's verbal productions. In our view, the more structured or specific the therapist's propositions are, the more information they supply to the patient as to what is expected of him.

It is our intention in this chapter to examine the effect of *therapist* informational structuring upon the level of patient verbal output and to examine the effect of *patient* output level upon therapist informational structure. In other words, we wish to find out whether and how the amount of specificity in therapist remarks influence or stimulate patient verbal productivity, and to analyze the effect of ample or diminished patient output upon therapist informational behavior.

THE INFORMATIONAL STRUCTURE OF THERAPIST VERBAL OUTPUT

In order to examine the overall informational structure of our therapists' verbal output in terms of degree of specificity, 64 sessions (the first eight hours of treatment for eight patients) were analyzed. The sample consisted of 5814 statements containing a total of 18,862 propositions. Each therapist statement was then classified according to the amount of structuring it imposed upon the patient, i.e., into one of eight categories of informational specificity.

Table 16 shows the percentage of each therapist's verbal output that falls into each category of informational stimulus value.

TABLE 16

INFORMATIONAL STRUCTURE OF THERAPIST VERBAL OUTPUT: PROPORTION OF THERAPIST STATEMENTS IN EACH OF EIGHT INFORMATIONAL CATEGORIES

Therapist informational categories	*Proportion of therapist statements* A	B	C	D	*Mean for all therapists*
1. Encourages passively	.06	.02	.16	.05	.06
2. Encourages actively	.04	.01	.03	.04	.03
3. Limits to subject matter area	.05	.03	.11	.16	.07
4. Limits to specific old proposition	.36	.28	.33	.22	.31
5. Limits to specific new proposition	.21	.40	.20	.28	.28
6. Interprets (redirects)	.19	.20	.04	.18	.16
7. Limits to specific answer	.08	.05	.12	.07	.08
8. Excludes discussion	.02	.004 [a]	.01 [a]	.01 [a]	.01

n = 5814 statements

[a] The actual number of statements in this category for these therapists was under 10.

It is interesting to note that the categories of informational specificity show a similar rank order among the therapists despite the differences the therapists manifest in activity level as measured by verbal output. Therapist C, one of the less active therapists, exhibits a propensity to use category (1) (passive encouragement) which constitutes 16 percent of his verbal output and avoids the use of category (6) (interpretation) which constitutes only 4 percent of his verbal output. Indeed, both of the less active therapists (C and D) make somewhat more use of the low-specificity categories (1), (2), and (3) than do the more active therapists.

Further research will be necessary to determine the extent to which the distribution of stimulus categories found in the present study is characteristic of psychotherapists in general, or is a function of different styles and techniques of psychotherapy, or is perhaps characteristic of the early life of therapy only. But one hypothesis would be that there are normative distributions of the informational stimulus categories which are specific to two-person therapeutic interactions. A second hypothesis would be that the distribution of informational categories is a function of the therapist's orientation and his style and technique of psychotherapy. If this were true, it might enable us to compare some of the differences among various schools of psychotherapy in quantitative terms. A third hypothesis of interest would be that other two-person communication systems (e.g., parent and child, teacher and student) if subjected to analysis in terms of the categories reported here would exhibit a similar informational structure.

INFORMATIONAL SEQUENCES IN PSYCHOTHERAPY

There has been considerable discussion among psychotherapists regarding when and for what purposes verbal responses of different informational specificity should be utilized in the course of therapy. For example, Sullivan expresses impatience with the lack of informational specificity characteristic of Freudian therapists:

> It is imperative, if you want to know where you are with another person, that you proceed along a path that he can at least dimly follow, so that he doesn't get lost completely as to what you are driving at. When he gets lost, very often you do too, and one or the other of you may not know it. The law of diminishing returns then begins to operate with great vigor without the patient's quite realizing it—and often without the psychiatrist's quite realizing it.

It is ideal, if you can, to go step by step with sufficient waving of signal flags, and so on so that there is always something approaching a consensus as to what is being discussed.[5]

Also from research on the interview and on small problem-solving groups come hypotheses about the consequences of varying degrees of directiveness for the maintenance of communication and the relation of group members to each other. Thus, with respect to the latter, Bales suggests that "The more directive and constrictive the quality of activity (*of one participant*), the more likely is it to arouse negative reactions (*in the other participant*)."[6]

The coding of therapist responses according to the system of categories developed for the present research enabled us to examine these problems quantitatively. The following questions can be asked of our data:

Do different categories of therapist response (high or low informational specificity) yield more or less quantity of patient verbal output?

Do different categories of therapist specificity yield more or less patient affect?

Do different categories of therapist specificity influence the continuity of the communication process during psychotherapy?

How does the level of the patient's verbal output influence the choice of informational category employed by the therapist?

THE EFFECTS OF THERAPIST INFORMATIONAL SPECIFICITY

(*a*) *Upon patient verbal output.* Since one of the initial and frequently recurring tasks undertaken by psychotherapists is to encourage their patients to verbalize, it will be of some interest to examine the effect of therapist informational tactics upon the extensiveness of patient verbal response. Patient verbalizations may be brief, consisting of a single proposition, or they may be quite extended, consisting of long sequences of propositions. Table 17 shows the relationship between specificity of therapist remarks and average number of propositions in the patient statement that follows (i.e., extensiveness). We notice that therapist statements containing propositions of low informational specificity consistently yield a greater number of patient propositions than do therapist statements containing propositions of high informational specificity, or in other words, patients talk more in response to therapist verbalizations of low structure. The average yield in patient propositions is 75

TABLE 17

THE EFFECT OF THERAPIST INFORMATIONAL SPECIFICITY ON PATIENT VERBAL OUTPUT: AVERAGE NUMBER OF PROPOSITIONS IN PATIENT STATEMENTS FOLLOWING EACH INFORMATIONAL CATEGORY

Therapist informational categories	*Average number of propositions in responsive statements of patients* A	B	C	D	*Mean for all patients*
1. Encourages passively	3.1	4.4	9.6	6.5	5.9
2. Encourages actively	22.1	7.9	3.8	7.4	10.3
3. Limits to subject matter area	5.5	10.8	12.0	18.8	11.8
4. Limits to specific old proposition	2.9	6.5	6.4	9.6	6.3
5. Limits to specific new proposition	2.4	4.7	5.7	7.7	5.1
6. Interprets (redirects)	2.3	3.7	5.7	4.6	4.1
7. Limits to specific answer	2.3	6.0	5.1	9.7	5.8
8. Excludes discussion	3.0	9.5[a]	2.5[a]	1.3[a]	4.1
Average yield of low-specificity categories (1) through (4)	6.8	4.6	8.1	12.4	7.0
Average yield of high-specificity categories (5) through (8)	4.5	2.4	4.4	6.8	4.0

n = 5814 statements

[a] The actual number of statements in this category for these therapists was under 10.

percent greater for the low than for the high informational categories.

Informational category (2) (active encouragement) and category (3) (limiting the patient to a subject matter area) seem to produce distinctly higher patient propositional yields than any of the other categories. In general, as therapist statements become more structured and more limiting in their stimulus value, they diminish the extensiveness of patient responses. Category (1) (passive encouragement) is most likely to be used when the patient is verbalizing actively (see Table 20) and it seems to serve the function of maintaining the level of patient verbal output. It is never used to stimulate verbalization when the patient is silent. It would appear then that patient verbal output is maximized when the therapist's activity imposes minimal limitation upon the content and direction of the patient's thought processes.

It should be realized, however, that the aspect of patient verbal output being measured here (average propositional yield per statement) does not fully reflect total patient output per session, nor take into account variations in rate of patient verbal output over time. One hypothesis which should be explored is that the frequency with which a therapist informational category is employed, as well as its effectiveness, is related to the phase of the session. For example, we suspect that the propositional yield for categories of low specificity will be higher at the beginning of the session than at other times during the session.

(*b*) *Upon patient affect.* Though maximization of patient verbalization is an important objective of therapy, the kind of information produced is regarded as no less important. For example, getting patients to verbalize about their feelings is also an important therapeutic objective.

Patient propositions were classified as to whether they referred to feelings (such as love, pleasure, or sadness) or not. Patient propositions such as "I feel like crying," and "I was glad that she wrote me" were coded as affective propositions.

If one extrapolated from the findings of small-group research, it would be expected that therapist responses of high informational specificity should result in an increased number of patient verbalizations of an affective sort. This assumption is not supported by the findings presented in Table 18. The findings also are not consistent among therapists when the results for the individual categories and the individual therapists are com-

TABLE 18

THE EFFECT OF THERAPIST INFORMATIONAL SPECIFICITY ON PATIENT OUTPUT OF AFFECTIVE PROPOSITIONS: PROPORTION OF PATIENT PROPOSITIONS THAT REFER TO AFFECT FOLLOWING EACH INFORMATIONAL CATEGORY

Therapist informational categories	*Proportion of patient propositions that refer to affect*				
	A	*B*	*C*	*D*	*All patients*
1. Encourages passively	.23	.28	.32	.05	.22
2. Encourages actively	.21	.28	.37	.14	.27
3. Limits to subject matter area	.21	.20	.20	.25	.21
4. Limits to specific old proposition	.22	.28	.19	.21	.23
5. Limits to specific new proposition	.20	.27	.19	.27	.23
6. Interprets (redirects)	.19	.29	.35	.26	.27
7. Limits to specific answer	.06	.14	.21	.15	.14
8. Excludes discussion	.16	.00 [a]	.09 [a]	.00 [a]	.06
Average yield of low-specificity categories (1) through (4)	.22	.27	.24	.21	.23
Average yield of high-specificity categories (5) through (8)	.17	.27	.22	.25	.23

n = 15,955 patient propositions

[a] This category is used less than 10 times by this therapist. Percentages for this category are probably not reliable.

pared. Category (6) (interpretation-redirection) does show a high yield of patient affective propositions for three of the four therapists. The highest affective yield for all categories and for all therapists results from the use of category (2) (active encouragement) by therapist C. Therapist B gets high affective yields from categories (1), (2), and (4). There appear to be no consistent trends among therapists with regard to which informational categories are most effective for the production of patient verbalization about affect. What works for one therapist does not always work for the others. This is in contrast to the consistency with which the categories are related to variations in patient verbal output (see Table 17).

(*c*) *Upon continuity of frame of reference.* Another desirable characteristic of therapeutic informational exchanges (as indeed of all communication), one upon which some investigators place a great deal of emphasis, is the appropriateness of a patient's reply or feedback. In a formal sense, a patient's response to a therapist's remarks may ordinarily (though not necessarily) be considered to be appropriate if drawn from the same subject matter area or frame of reference as the statement of the therapist. Continuance of the terms of reference by the patient constitutes a sort of consensual validation of effective communication between therapist and patient, because it signifies that at least there is agreement between them as to *what* they are communicating about.

For the purpose of approaching this problem quantitatively, eight subject matter or content classes were developed. Each proposition was then classified and coded into one of the eight reference systems, according to its terms of reference (e.g., the self, the treatment, the family). For example, a proposition like "Isn't a therapist able to tell me a thing like this?" was coded as having the treatment as its frame of reference. A proposition like "My father yelled at me today" was coded as being drawn from the family frame of reference.

By identifying the reference category of a patient response, it was possible to get a rough estimate of the relevance of the response to the preceding therapist communication. Each patient statement was then examined to see if it fell into the same or a different frame of reference from that of the therapist statement that preceded it. Identity of system categories between statements was treated as evidence that communication regarding a given content was continuing, while a difference in categories between statements was regarded as an indication that a change in subject had been introduced.

TABLE 19

THE EFFECT OF THERAPIST INFORMATIONAL SPECIFICITY ON CONSISTENCY OF FRAME OF REFERENCE: FREQUENCY OF PATIENT CHANGE OF SYSTEM REFERENT

Therapist informational categories	*Proportion of patient statements that begin with a change in referent*				*Mean for all patients*
	A	*B*	*C*	*D*	
Average subject change yield of low-specificity categories (1) through (4)	.06	.07	.07	.10	.08
Average subject change yield of high-specificity categories (5) through (8)	.05	.04	.03	.06	.04

n = 5814 statements

Table 19 shows the proportion of patient statements that had frames of reference different from those of the therapist statements that preceded them. For each therapist, a smaller proportion of subject matter changes by patients follows statements of high specificity than follows statements of low informational specificity. On the average, subject matter change by patients following therapist statements of high informational specificity is only one-half as frequent as after therapist communications of low informational specificity.

The findings suggest that for moving communication along a coherent and consistent path, there is an advantage in employing categories of high informational specificity. On the other hand, when seeking new subject matter areas for exploration and for transferring the initiative to the patient, probes of low informational specificity appear to be useful. The findings also constitute a validation of the informational categories themselves, as they have now been shown to limit the array of responses from which patients select their replies. The probability that the patient will draw from a new frame of reference diminishes with the rise in therapist informational specificity.

THE EFFECT OF VARIATIONS IN THE LEVEL OF PATIENT VERBAL OUTPUT ON THE INFORMATIONAL STRUCTURE OF THERAPIST RESPONSES

Assuming that one of the important functions performed by psychotherapists is to maintain or to increase the level of patient verbal output, one may profitably examine the effects of change in patient verbal output on the informational tactics of psychotherapists. The present research is based upon a model of psychotherapy as an informational exchange system, and the behavior of the participants is described in terms of the quality and quantity of information transmitted. Informational input and output are assumed to be systematically interrelated. We anticipated that variations in or cessation of patient verbal output (i.e., silence) would bring about changes in the characteristics of the therapist's verbal input of such a nature as to restore the flow of communication between the participants.

Patient behavior was classified into three categories: (1) high verbal output, i.e., lengthy statements, consisting of more than three propositions, (2) low verbal output, i.e., brief statements, consisting of three or less propositions, and (3) absence of verbalization, i.e., silence of 10 or more seconds.

Hypotheses

(1) Therapy constitutes an informational exchange system. As the output of information from the patient diminishes, the output of information from the therapist is expected to increase so as to maintain the system. With respect to the variables considered here, this would mean that a decrease in quantity of patient verbalization would serve to increase the specificity of therapist response.

(2) Since silence represents the limiting and most clear-cut case of decreased patient informational output, it should tend to maximize the informational output of the therapist (e.g., his specificity).

(3) Silence is an interruption in the flow of communication during psychotherapy. It may be the result of lack of consensus in the expectations of the patient and therapist as to the direction of communication flow. It may also be interpreted as a patient's temporary inability or unwillingness to verbalize. When therapists interrupt silences, they should therefore be expected to employ informational behavior that tends to clarify communicational expectations and to stimulate patient verbal output.

The question form is peculiarly suited for the clarification of communicational expectations and for the transfer of the initiative from one to the other member of a communicational dyad. Through the use of the question form, any lack of consensus between two persons as to who is expected to speak is resolved, since a question is an explicit verbalization that the questioner expects the other to speak. The use of questions by therapists would therefore be one of the logical means by which patient silences could be terminated. In accordance with this expectation, we examined our data on therapist use of the interrogatory form. We compared the frequency of its use in response to patient silence with the frequency of its use in response to patient verbalization. We found that the proportion of therapist statements in the question form rises from 33 percent after verbalization to 53 percent after patient silences.

COMPARISON OF THERAPIST RESPONSE TO PATIENT VERBALIZATION WITH THERAPIST RESPONSE TO PATIENT SILENCES

Table 20 shows the effect of variations in the level of patient verbal output upon the therapists' use of the eight informational categories relating to specificity. We are comparing the column in Table 20 reading "all patient statements" with the column reading "patient silences." It will be seen that the frequency with which therapists employ the eight informational categories changes considerably as patient verbal output falls. In general, as patient output falls, therapists tend to increase the amount of information in their verbalizations. Whereas after lengthy patient statements only 48 percent of therapist propositions fall into the four highest specificity categories, after brief patient statements 58 percent fall into these categories, and after patient silences, 69 percent.[7] Thus the general hypothesis (that as patient output of information falls, therapists tend to increase the amount of information they feed into the therapeutic interaction) is supported by the findings.

Therapists respond to silence by entirely eliminating category (1) (passive encouragement) responses. They also markedly decrease the frequency with which they employ category (4) (refers patient to specific old proposition). These two categories ordinarily constitute 37 percent of therapist output but after patient silence they constitute only 11 percent of therapist output. On the other hand, considerable increases are shown in the utilization of category (2) (active encouragement), category

(5) (introduces specific new proposition), and category (8) (excludes further discussion). These three categories together ordinarily account for only 32 percent of therapist verbal output, but they constitute 61 percent of therapist output following patient silence. Though the general trend toward specificity is conspicuous in therapist response to silence, even the variations can be seen to comprise a coherent pattern of response if one assumes that the therapists are reacting to silences not only as the limiting case of diminished patient output but also as though silence signaled a termination of a communication sequence or cycle.

The hypothesis that therapists regard silence as an indication that an informational phase in the session should be closed is supported by their increased use of category (8) (excludes further discussion). Moreover, therapists markedly decrease their use of category (4) (refers to specific old proposition) and increase their use of category (5) (introduces specific new proposition).

We have now seen that variations in the level of patient output affect the informational structure of therapist communication. Therapists react differently when their patient is verbalizing freely than when their patients are temporarily silent.

COMPARISON OF THERAPIST RESPONSE TO LENGTHY PATIENT STATEMENTS WITH THERAPIST RESPONSE TO BRIEF PATIENT STATEMENTS

We wanted to quantify further "level of patient output." The unit of quantity used in the present study was the "proposition" and quantity of verbal output was defined as "number of propositions." "Verbalizing freely" expresses the idea of a high rate of verbal output. But does this mean that the patient speaks frequently, or that he speaks extensively each time he speaks? A survey of our data on total patient verbal output per session suggested that frequent and rapid interaction between therapist and patient was just as likely to account for high patient verbal output for the session as a whole as were lengthy patient verbalizations. In fact, brief patient verbalizations may be correlated with total verbal output for the whole session.

We investigated the effect of low-output statements on thera-

TABLE 20

THE LEVEL OF PATIENT VERBAL OUTPUT AND THE INFORMATIONAL STRUCTURE OF THERAPIST RESPONSE

Therapist informational categories	*Proportion of therapist responses following:* All patient statements	Lengthy[a] patient statements	Brief[b] patient statements	Patient silences
(1) Encourages passively	.06	.07	.05	.00
(2) Encourages actively	.03	.03	.03	.09
(3) Refers to subject matter area	.07	.13	.05	.11
(4) Refers to specific old proposition	.31	.29	.29	.11
(5) Introduces specific new proposition	.28	.25	.30	.43
(6) Interprets (redirects)	.16	.11	.19	.11
(7) Limits to specific answer	.08	.10	.08	.06
(8) Excludes discussion	.01	.02	.01	.09
Responses in low-specificity categories (1) through (4)	.47	.52	.42	.31
Responses in high-specificity categories (5) through (8)	.53	.48	.58	.69[c]

n = 5814 statements

[a] Statements consisting of more than three propositions
[b] Statements consisting of one to three propositions
[c] Chi-square significant at .001 level

pist responses. This was done by comparing the informational structure of therapist output after brief patient statements (consisting of one to three propositions) with therapist output after lengthy patient statements (containing more than three propositions).

Table 20 shows the effect of low- and high-output patient

statements on therapist informational specificity. It can be seen that there is a definite trend toward greater therapist specificity following brief patient statements. However, there appears to be a slightly different pattern of response by our therapists to low output than to silence. Interpretations [category (6)] are more frequent as are references to previous ideas [category (4)]. Both silences and brief verbalizations call forth more therapist informational specificity. Silence, however, tends to terminate a communicational cycle, while brief patient statements signal continued interest and exploration in depth.

Let us briefly utilize the findings concerning the interrelation between patient verbalization (its absence or presence and extent) and specificity of therapist response, and on the basis of our results, let us suggest the character of informational equilibrium tendencies in therapy. Schematically, the extrapolation of our findings is presented in Fig. 11.

An episode of high patient output (extensive patient verbalization) may be initiated by low structuring therapist behavior and may be maintained by such behavior. In the case of a radical decrease in patient verbalization or temporary inability to verbalize, highly specific interventions are required to overcome communicational inertia. The communications immediately following such a maneuver will more likely be classifiable as medium rather than as high output. It is by such a maneuver that the process can again be set into full motion; an informational equilibrium is restored through sequences of high patient output and low structuring therapist behavior.[8]

SUMMARY

The transmission and feedback of information are the means through which therapeutic systems achieve their adaptational goals. One major objective of psychotherapy is to maximize the amount of information available to the patient. In this chapter, we examined the effect of the structure of the therapist's infor-

FIGURE 11

EXTRAPOLATION OF INFORMATIONAL SYSTEM TRENDS

Therapist	*Patient*	*Therapist*	*Patient*
LOW SPECIFICITY ⟶	*HIGH OUTPUT* ⟶ [mean = 7.0 patient propositions per therapist statement]	*LOW SPECIFICITY* ⟶	*HIGH OUTPUT*
HIGH SPECIFICITY ⟶	*MEDIUM OUTPUT* ⟶ [mean = 4.0 patient propositions per therapist statement]	*LOW SPECIFICITY* ⟶	*HIGH OUTPUT*
	LOW OUTPUT ⟶ [mean = 1–3 patient propositions per therapist statement]	*HIGH SPECIFICITY* ⟶	*MEDIUM OUTPUT*
	ABSENCE OF OUTPUT ⟶ [silence]	*HIGH SPECIFICITY* ⟶	*MEDIUM OUTPUT*

mational output upon the patient's informational output, and vice versa.

A system of categories was developed to estimate the amount of specificity in therapist propositions. The use by the therapist of different categories was found to be related to patient output. Low-specificity statements consistently yielded a greater number of patient propositions than high-specificity statements, while high-specificity reduced the likelihood that patients would change the topic under discussion. As patient output falls, therapist specificity increases. In other words, therapists feed more information into the system when patient output falls and less information into the system when patient output is high.

It appears as if the informational system in psychotherapy also imposes its own system characteristics upon the informational behavior of both patient and therapist. These subsystem requirements dealing with the maintenance of optimum levels of output exhibit their own dynamic which is relatively autonomous and which to some extent transcends the specific adaptational goals of the therapy system, the diagnosis of the patient, and the theoretical orientation of the therapists.

NOTES

1. Ruesch, *Disturbed Communication*, p. 6.
2. Sullivan, *Conceptions of Modern Psychiatry*, p. 90.
3. *Ibid.*
4. Menninger, *Theory of Psychoanalytic Technique*, p. 27.
5. Sullivan, *The Psychiatric Interview*, p. 46.
6. Parsons, Bales, and Shils, *Working Papers in the Theory of Action.*
7. These differences are significant at the .001 level.
8. The remarks above represent a model of the process based upon the results reported here. Since we did not have a scheme whereby we could classify propositions in the form of particular

sequences, we cannot state how precisely the model presented in the figure approximates trends existing in our data. This kind of a task awaits future researchers in this area. We feel, however, that the kind of analysis reported here has indicated the significance of such efforts as well as provided some tools for their implementation.

Part Four

THERAPY AS A SYSTEM OF ROLE EXPECTATIONS

CHAPTER VII

The Dimensions of Therapist and Patient Role Expectations

In this chapter, we shall identify some of the dimensions in terms of which patient and therapist role expectations can be dissected. We shall then describe some of the specific components into which these dimensions can be analyzed. We shall also attempt to determine the degree of similarity in the expectations of our therapists and patients with respect to these components.

When both members of a dyad are in agreement regarding their reciprocal obligations and returns, there is consensus or similarity of expectations, and harmony or stability occurs in their interpersonal relations.[1] The system is then said to be in equilibrium. But when there is any degree of discrepancy or lack of consensus between the participants, and their expectations are dissimilar, the role system is disequilibriated and manifestations of strain appear in their interpersonal relations. If expectations are too dissimilar, the social system disintegrates unless the differences can be reconciled.

In the two chapters that follow, we will show that when there is dissimilarity in therapist-patient role expectations, such dissimilarity has specific consequences upon the structure of the communication that takes place during therapy.

Since, in a sense, expectations are "rules" governing behavior, we turned our attention to those behaviors inherent in the process of interacting and communicating for which "rules" are needed. The problems of verbal communication in a two-person group may be resolved into four specific components: who shall speak, how much, about what, and when? "When" has a double meaning as used here, i.e., "when" meaning when in time (who shall speak, how much, and about what)? and "when" meaning under what circumstances (who shall speak, how much, and about what)? "Who," "what," and "how much" are thus seen to be functions not only of time, but also of circumstances.

EXPECTATIONS REGARDING ACTIVENESS

The first two problems of communicating, "Who shall speak?" and "How much?," will be recognized as components of the dimension we have previously referred to as "activeness." Expectations governing behavior along this dimension will be referred to as "activeness expectations." Patient and therapist activeness expectations pertain to the following issues: (1) Who should take the initiative in communicating?; (2) How frequently should they speak?; (3) To what extent should the therapist direct the patient as to what he should talk about?; (4) How "directive" should the therapist be with regard to the patient's activities outside of therapy?; (5) Should the therapist give advice and counsel?; and (6) How much explanation about therapy should the therapist provide?

We found that our patients and their therapists all agreed in their initial expectations that patient and therapist roles are asymmetrical with respect to relative amount of activeness. All eleven of the patients in the original sample anticipated that they would do most of the talking during psychotherapy, and the four therapists concurred.

However, when we compared therapist and patient expectations regarding the more specific components of activeness listed above, we found a considerable amount of disagreement in expectations. The number of disagreements (out of six questions) per therapist-patient pair ranged from one to five, with an average of three disagreements.[2] These differences in expectations became a recurrent topic of discussion during therapy and this was reflected in the subject matter and structure of the communications that took place. The ways in which these expectational disequilibria were resolved will be treated in subsequent chapters.

Complementary expectations regarding activeness are required to regulate human interactions. When we use this concept in connection with psychotherapy, we have in mind expectations regarding the initiative, responsibility, and control of communication during treatment. In our view, successful maintenance of all major role relationships involves definition of expectations with regard to activeness. Failure to achieve reciprocity in this area is a major source of strain in social systems. Consider, for example, the marital relationship in which there is disagreement about the rules governing the allocation of initiative and responsibility; or a teacher-student situation in which the student does not expect to assume as much responsibility as the teacher expects (or the teacher assumes a more passive role than the student expects). Parents' activeness expectations regarding children are often very neatly packaged in common sayings, such as, "Children should be seen but not heard," and "Speak only when spoken to."

In the course of his socialization during treatment, the patient is helped to achieve more expectational consensus with his therapist, and expectational dissimilarity and disequilibrium are accordingly reduced. Of course, in line with Bateson's deutero-learning idea, more than mere consensus in expectations is achieved. The patient also learns the instrumental acts and contingencies of role learning itself. The not inconsiderable effort expended in therapy in teaching the patient the relative distribution of responsibilities, initiative, and control is rewarded both by a facilitation of the process within therapy and by more adequate functioning without.

EXPECTATIONS REGARDING SELECTIVITY

The third problem in communicating requires decisions as to relevance and irrelevance, decisions "about what" to communicate. Expectations in this dimension concern what subject matters are considered to be significant and relevant for discussion during psychotherapy. It is naturally to be assumed that what the participants expect to talk about will influence what they actually do talk about. Expectations that select from among equiprobable subjects for communication are subsumed under the dimension of selectivity.[3]

Therapist and patient expectations regarding selectivity were tapped by questions about (1) which subject matters are considered to be very relevant, somewhat relevant, or not at all relevant; and (2) by questions on whether distinctions between relevant and nonrelevant material were to be made at all. The answers given by the therapists and patients were combined into indices of selectivity.[4] If the therapist or the patient set specific priorities upon subject matters, we classified them as high in selectivity. If they exhibited no preference among potential subject matters, we classified them as low in selectivity. The therapists and patients disagreed as to the relevance of about one-half of the subject matter areas about which they were asked. The differences were due in the main to the fact that the therapists consistently ranked lower in selectivity than their patients. In other words, patients are more apt to expect to exclude certain subject matters from discussion, as if they expected psychotherapy to be a relationship which was limited in content and purpose; while the therapists tended to admit a broader array of topics into their purview as to what was relevant to the therapeutic relationship.

As we shall see in the next chapter, it was difficult for the patients to abandon their view that the therapeutic relationship should be restricted to a discussion of what they conceived as their "problem." The basic requirement of verbalization without restraint was violated by the patient's conscious selection among alternate subject matter areas. The problem is nicely formulated in a patient's reverie in a short story by Mary McCarthy:

> . . . what if it *were important* and she failed to tell him? What if her reluctance to delay over a trifle really masked an unconscious fear? In this room, you never knew whether you were putting obstacles in the way or clearing the path. It was a *question of relevance*, but how could you determine what was *relevant to the Unknown?* [5]

One of the essential things that a patient is required to learn about the "what" of therapeutic communication is that he must abandon any preconceptions he may have regarding selectivity.

Definitions regarding appropriateness and inappropriateness of subject matter areas are involved in all role relationships. For instance, it is interesting to note that, as in therapy, there exist in the parent-child role relationship reciprocal expectations to the effect that the child should communicate everything to the parent while the parent may limit what he communicates to a child. When the adolescent child begins to become selective in his communications to his parents, he often finds himself at variance with his parents' selectivity expectations. Likewise, a wife's inquiry about "what is new at the office" may not fit her husband's selectivity expectations.

Part of the process of learning "about what" to communicate in therapy is for the patient to unlearn what he thought he was supposed to talk about, and to become sensitive in expectational terms to the requirements of the situation in which he finds himself. The hypothesis of deutero-learning in role behavior is again applicable here. Not only does the therapeutic interaction help in learning how to learn role expectations, but it also helps the patient to learn how to *unlearn* them.

EXPECTATIONS REGARDING DIFFERENTIATION

The problem of "when" to communicate is of a somewhat different order than the previous problems of "who," "how much," and "about what." Thus far we have stated that at any given time T, expectations govern the communicational behavior of the participants in any interaction with reference to "who," "how much," and "about what." But, in its temporal meaning, the "when" of communication refers to the expectations of the participants as to the "who," "how much," and "about what" at various times T_1, T_2, T_3, . . . T_n. For example, therapists expect in general that they are more likely to offer interpretations near the end of a therapeutic session, and that they are more likely to offer interpretations later in therapy than in the early sessions. Expectations such as these, which are contingent upon time, will be referred to as "expectations regarding temporal differentiation." These are expectations regarding the variation of behavior through time.

To inquire into these expectations, we devised a series of questions to determine the degree of temporal differentiation in each therapist's role expectations. In an attempt to arrive at the therapist's expectations regarding variation of his performance, we asked: (1) *When* in therapy (within the session as well as over therapy) would he expect to say more than a few words?; (2) During what stages of therapy would he be more likely to provide reassurance, support, etc.? While therapists do not fully agree on when they would be more likely to speak, they nevertheless all definitely expect to vary the amounts and kinds of their verbal behavior in relation to the length of time the system or subsystem persists.

Most of the patients in our sample show some awareness of

this aspect of differentiation of therapist behavior in their answers to our questions. Their expectations, however, lack the clarity of the therapists' expectations, and as we will see in the subsequent chapter, this lack of clarity is reflected in their verbal behavior.

A sense of *when* behavior of a given kind is appropriate is required for adequate functioning in all role relationships. For example, when can a friend feel free to share his troubles? When may a young suitor expect his first kiss? In the family constellation, expectations as to the children's behavior are constantly revised as their ages change. Many petty conflicts between parents and their children arise from changing expectations regarding activeness that are not shared by the participants, e.g., "You are old enough now to take some responsibility." Perhaps no other single factor is more responsible for parental disappointment and frustration with children than expectations that are out of phase with time. Differential expectations regarding children of different ages in the same family (which remain unexplained and unexplored) may lead to sibling rivalry problems. Here we may have a very interesting complex of dissimilarity in the expectations of a whole family leading to tension and strain in their social relations.

Failure in reciprocity may be due to the assumption of "who," "how much," and "about what," at the wrong time. In learning about differentiation while in therapy, the patient becomes more sensitive to the unfolding of patterns in relationships in general, and he learns that movement toward a goal in interpersonal relationships requires different actions at different times.

The "when" of communication can also be interpreted as meaning "under what circumstances" shall "who speak," "how much," "about what." If the expectational emphasis is upon the variation that will occur in behavior depending upon the *situation* rather than upon the *duration* of the relationship, then we can speak of "expectations regarding situational differentiation."

Expectations covered by this concept refer to how "consistently" or how "differently" a therapist expects to behave depending upon the patient's situational status. For instance, does he plan to act differently when a patient is depressed than when he is agitated? Or, for example, does a patient expect to be given reassurance under certain circumstances and not under others?

Patients and therapists have expectations exhibiting clear-cut ideas about situational differentiation. Patients seem to be more familiar with situational differentiation than with temporal differentiation. Consequently, their expectations concerning situational differentiation are clearer than their expectations regarding temporal differentiation. Patients are more aware of the requirement for situational differentiation probably because it involves a phenomenon occurring at only one point in time. This may be tied to early socialization experience, which abounds in examples of "situational differentiation." Children learn, for example, that parents respond differently to them when they are hurt than when they have done some mischief.

EXPECTATIONS REGARDING PROGRESS AND DURATION OF TREATMENT

The fourth dimension of expectations which was given attention, while it does not deal with any specific problem of communication, does involve expectations that bear on the problem of maintenance of the system as a whole. It concerns expectations regarding how long treatment will take and how long it will take before any progress can be expected. We shall call this dimension "timing." Timing refers to therapist and patient expectations as to the total duration of their relationship and the time required to accomplish specific goals short of fulfilling all of the purposes for which the relationship was undertaken.

Specifically, this dimension refers to therapist and patient expectations as to how long the patient will be in therapy and as to how long it will take the patient to lose this or that symptom for which therapy had been sought. Information about therapist and patient expectations regarding the "pace" at which therapy would proceed was gathered by asking the therapist and patient about how soon they expected to have made some progress in therapy toward the management of the patient's problems. Differences in therapist and patient progress expectations seemed to be crucial in the termination or continuance of the therapy relationship. There were two patients in our original sample who expected to make some progress within the first few weeks of therapy. In each of these cases, the therapists did not expect progress to be made until after the fourth month of therapy. One of the patients terminated treatment after the third session and the other after the seventh session! On the other hand, the two patients who expected progress to take place later than anticipated by their therapists were both still in treatment after 18 months.

However, many patients who expected progress to be made somewhat earlier than did their therapists also remained in treatment. This is not surprising since therapists are aware of the possibility of dissimilarity in therapist-patient expectations regarding progress and duration of treatment and they ordinarily bend their efforts toward modifying patients' timing expectations. While dissimilarities in timing expectations appear to be generic to the therapeutic relationship, therapy is not the only role relationship for which an analysis of expectations in terms of a "timing" factor is relevant. It appears to us that it is relevant to the initial and crucial phases of many role relationships. For example, an employee must learn what accomplishments are expected of him within specified periods of time.

Timing expectations transcend role expectations in that they bear directly upon the problems of illness, cure, and progress in general. Davis's[6] work on polio patients and Roth's[7] comments on tuberculosis patients illustrate the importance of this concept in the "sociology of medicine." Davis, for example, showed how polio patients socialized in the norms of the rehabilitation culture may be well satisfied with being able to make a few additional muscle movements after a week's or a month's effort, but parents' reaction of disappointment with such "minor" progress may easily interfere with the child's continuing acceptance of the institutional norms of progress.

In the next chapter, it will be seen that discussion revolving around the problem of "timing" arises in therapy irrespective of the theoretical orientation of the therapist, the diagnosis, or the complaint of the patient.

NOTES

1. Spiegel, "The Resolution of Role Conflict within the Family," *The Patient and the Mental Hospital*, ed. by Greenblatt, Levinson, and Williams.

2. The six questions are:

Will the therapist—

suggest what to talk about next?
prohibit the patient from doing things he considers inadvisable?
counsel or advise the patient on the management of day-to-day living?
explain what therapy is all about?
reassure the patient and be sympathetic when he feels depressed or unhappy?
discuss politics and other issues of the day with the patient?

3. This dimension of selectivity is similar to Parsons's classification of roles along a *specificity-diffuseness* axis. In Parsons's scheme, professional role relationships would all be characterized as functionally specific. Family relationships would comprise an example of functionally diffuse relationships.

4. In scoring therapist or patient expectations regarding selec-

tivity, the particular subject matter was not scored; only whether it was considered relevant or not was scored.

5. McCarthy, "Ghostly Father I Confess," *The Company She Keeps,* p. 187.

6. Davis, "Definitions of Time and Recovery in Paralytic Polio Convalescence," *American Journal of Sociology,* LXI (No. 6, May, 1956), 582–587.

7. Roth, "The Time Table of the T.B. Patient," unpublished manuscript.

Part Five

INTERRELATIONS BETWEEN COMMUNICATION AND EXPECTATIONS

CHAPTER VIII

Expectations and Behavior in Therapy

We have suggested, as a minimum, that a social system be conceived of as involving two subsystems, that of communication and that of expectations. Each system can be treated separately from the other and this is what we have done so far. We will now take up some of the interrelations between the systems of expectation and communication. We will try to document the hypothesis that asymmetry in the system of expectations (dissimilarities in role expectations) is reflected in asymmetry in the system of communication (communicational strain), and we will try to show how efforts are made in the latter system to resolve strain created by the former.

The documentation provided in this chapter for the interdependence between systems is not quantitative but is in the form of specific verbalizations dealing with discrepancies in expectations. In this way, we can show that the dimensions discussed in the previous chapter are far from mere theoretical constructs and that they relate in a very real sense to the content of "therapeutic" learning. The material presented in this chapter, therefore, consists of excerpts of therapeutic communication. In the succeeding chapter, we will re-examine with quantitative tools the interrelationship between expectation and communication.

EFFECT OF DISSIMILARITIES IN THERAPIST-PATIENT EXPECTATIONS UPON THE CONTENT OF COMMUNICATION

We will first introduce a set of quotations consisting of patient verbalizations which reflect unfulfilled (dissimilar) expectations in order to see how patients express their experience with a given expectational problem. Then in a series of subsequent excerpts we will show how therapists through their communication attempt to resolve the problem faced by the patients as a result of dissimilarity in expectations. Episodes of strain and role-teaching similar to these recur again and again throughout therapy.

1. *Expectations Regarding Activeness*

Patient Statements of Expectational Problem:

Patient: A couple of seconds ago, uh, there was a silence in which I had nothing to say or I didn't say anything. And just before you said something I thought of this fact that, uh, I wonder *who's* going to talk first and *why*.

Patient: I was trying to arrive at a couple of things (*sigh*). The reaction of the analyst sitting and just staring at me, and waiting for me to say something or to think of something leads to two kinds of feelings in me. One, instead of coming forth and being able to think of things, is that I either draw a blank or, uh, have to fight to try and almost make up things to fill the void.

Patient: Well, actually, I haven't found this, uh, the kind of experience that I've anticipated. It's rather frustrating. It's difficult for me to carry on a one-man conversation with myself, something I've never been able to do.

Patient: I thought, uh, there would be more of a, uh, interaction, back and forth in trying to at least, get at your reactions to the kind of feeling I have.

Therapist Role Definition Responses:

Therapist: You would like some reactions from me, is that it?
Patient: In a sense, yes.
Therapist: Why?

Patient: Well, what is the relationship we have? Is it, do I get reactions from you or do I, what kind of a, an emotional learning process takes place if there is no reaction from you? I really don't know. Can I learn just by hearing myself?

Therapist: Look, it's easy for me to tell you some answers so you will know how you should behave. . . . That way we don't find out anything about your motivations, your thinking, your emotions.

Therapist: Well, why don't we take it easy and wait till something occurs to you. We don't have to fill every second with sound.

Patient: . . . I suppose after a while it gets to be a game to see who can outstare the other.

Therapist: Is that what it feels like?

Patient: Well, I am trying to bring a humorous element into it.

Therapist: Hmm, that is a very difficult aspect of it though. It's sort of to get used to the nothing . . . that you're gonna come in and the doctor will just wait . . . he'd like to hear . . . what you have on your mind.

Therapist: No, that's what I hope you'll learn to do if you keep coming in, just sort of ramble on and let me try to—

Patient: Make sense out of it.

Therapist: Not to try to make sense, there'll be a lot of sense in it, but try to develop a sort of *pattern* or something like it.

2. *Expectations Regarding Selectivity*

Patient Statements of the Expectational Problem:

Patient: All right now, would you say that I should try to talk about mostly what happens nowadays or mostly about whether it relates back?

Patient: Yeah, I don't know. Ah, well, I don't know what to talk about, I mean.

Patient: I am just thinking whether—what you're waiting for me to say?

Therapist Role Definition Responses:

Patient: I guess it's generally your policy to have your patient talk as much as he wants and as freely as he wants.

Therapist: Well, the procedure is generally that you lie down and relax on the couch, and then put all your feelings, your memories, and your thoughts, into words so far as you can.

Patient: With no direction?

Therapist: With no direction and preferably with no selection. I know this is impossible, but so far as you can, you let me be the judge about what's important and what's not important. You just come in open-mindedly and report the data.

Patient: That's quite a thought, considering the data in any person's life takes up twenty-four hours every day.

Therapist: Well, since you needn't select, just say what's on top of your head.

Patient: . . . I can't think of anything else that you'd be interested in.

Therapist: Talk about something that *you* would be interested in.

Patient: Nothing that would be significant in psychotherapy—

Therapist: Well, nothing that happens to you is insignificant in terms of our trying to get to know you, whether it's by accident or by design, whatever happens and what effects it has on you—

Patient: Yeah.

Therapist: —helps us to understand.

Patient: (35-*second pause*) That's all I can think of now.

Therapist: Talk about anything else that you want to. Any you listed as problems last time. You may want to go into detail with respect to some of them or take some other points up. I want you to feel free to talk about anything.

3. *Expectations Regarding Temporal and Situational Differentiation*

Patient Statements of the Expectational Problem:

Patient: I wonder when, when you're going to, uh, start getting rough with me, probe—

Therapist: Speak with authority.

Patient: Yeah, speak with authority and, uh, bat me around a little bit, uh, snipe at me. Catch me up on things I say. So far the soliloquies I've indulged in—hasn't uncovered anything. (temporal)

Patient: I was thinking too that in the beginning you never said anything or occasionally a little "mm-hm" or "hmm." But now, ah, you're entering in more from a conversational viewpoint. (temporal)

Patient: I thought you'd be more sympathetic than you usually are, when you saw how upset I was. (situational)

Therapist Role Definition Responses:

Therapist: I want to say something about me. You may ask any question you wish, but I may not answer them. I answer only those questions that I think are to your advantage to hear answers to, and I delay answering all others until such time as I feel it is appropriate. (temporal)

Therapist: I wish I could give you the answer right now, but it wouldn't do you any good if I presented you with an answer right now. (temporal)

4. *Expectations Regarding Timing*

Patient Statements of the Expectational Problem:

Patient: No, I know that it will take quite a bit of time. But I was just hoping that I'd be started on the way to helping myself, improving these things. I really don't seem to know what I expect now. But I know it will take quite a bit of time.

Patient: I know you say you have to sorta sneak up on this thing, but I don't know. It's hard for me to grasp hold of that idea.

Therapist Role Definition Responses:

Patient: I don't know, sometimes I feel so disgusted, I just feel like forgetting about the whole thing.

Therapist: That's what I mean. That's what I meant last time when I said it might take you a while to sort of get over the discouragement of feeling that pschotherapy is going to be something that's going to take *time and work.*

Therapist: Oh, I think you understand it very well, but it's just that I think you're kind of reluctant to accept it—because it means sort of that you're not going to be able to have a quick answer to all your problems.

Therapist: Well, this takes a good deal of time. Go slowly. What did you expect to get out of psychotherapy? And how fast did you expect to go? . . . Sometimes it takes months before you get anything out of this, because you can't hurry this along. You have, did you think that after a few visits, the heavens would open—

Patient: No.

Therapist:—as they do in the movies or in the short stories, and all your problems will be solved?

In this chapter, we have examined the content of communication in therapy and we have seen how patients voice their expectational confusion and how therapists attempt to resolve it, though we have not yet undertaken a quantitative appraisal of frequency and variation in these phenomena. In the next chapter, we undertake to reformulate the problems of expectational dissimilarity and its effects upon communication in quantitative terms. We will construct operational tools which will enable us to gauge the *degree* of dissimilarity of expectations and the effect of varying amounts of dissimilarity upon therapist management of the primary system.

CHAPTER IX

Expectations and Initial Communication

This chapter deals with the effect that therapist and patient expectations have upon subsequent therapist-patient communication. In contrast to the preceding chapter, the appraisal reported here is quantitative. We shall first examine therapist initial expectations regarding activeness and the relationship of these expectations to actual communication.

THERAPIST EXPECTATIONS REGARDING ACTIVENESS

To get at the therapists' activeness self-images and to assess their activeness expectations, each therapist was asked in a pre-therapy interview whether they considered themselves to be primarily an active or a passive participant in the therapeutic situation. They were asked, in general, how frequently they spoke during treatment. We have summarized their replies to these questions in Table 21. As can be seen, the responses to the questions place the therapists in about the same rank order for activeness. Activeness in the quantitative sense used here should not be confused with the issue of "directiveness." Activeness merely refers to the amount of verbal activity that the therapist engages in, not to the content of such verbal participation. Directiveness bears the connotation of direction and control over the patient's activities outside of therapy and often subsumes such categories of activities as value judgements, advice, and prescription.

Table 22 shows that there is a consistent relationship between the therapists' expectations as to how verbally active they would be, and their actual verbal activity during treatment as measured by the following three indices of activeness:

1. *Therapist Verbal Output:* This is defined as the number of therapist propositions in any given session or group of sessions. It is a measure of the *absolute* volume of the therapist's contribution.

TABLE 21

THERAPIST RESPONSES TO QUESTIONS DEALING WITH THEIR ACTIVENESS IN THERAPY

Therapist	*Active or passive participant*	*Frequency of speaking*
A	"Very active"	"Will speak a great deal depending on circumstances"
B	"Active in a nondirective sense"	"Somewhat less frequently than in ordinary conversation"
C	"Passive"	"Very infrequently"
D	"More Passive"	"Very infrequently"

2. *Therapist Proportion of Verbal Output:* This is defined as the number of therapist propositions divided by the total number of propositions obtained in a single session or group of sessions. It is a measure of the therapist's proportion of verbal activity during treatment and is one means of quantifying therapist-patient role differentiation.

3. *Rate of Interaction:* This is defined as the average number of exchanges or interactions that occur per session or per transcribed page, and it tells us how *often* the therapist speaks.

Thus our therapists were found to have a fairly clear and consistent conception of how verbally active they would be during treatment. Because these estimates of activeness were made prior to contact with the patients, and because inter-therapist variance in activity level was greater than inter-patient variance, it follows that at least in the early stages of therapy verbal activeness of therapists is largely (though obviously not entirely) a function of their experience and role

TABLE 22
THERAPISTS' CONCEPTION OF ACTIVENESS AND THEIR VERBAL OUTPUT DURING THE FIRST EIGHT SESSIONS OF TREATMENT

	Quantitative measures of verbal activity		
Therapists in rank order of self-ratings on activeness	*Average number of propositions per session*	*Proportion of total verbal output*	*Mean number of interactions per session*
Therapist A:			
Patient 1	136	.30	78
Patient 2	166	.36	115
Mean	151	.33	96
Therapist B:			
Patient 1	114	.25	79
Patient 2	97	.21	61
Mean	106	.23	70
Therapist C:			
Patient 1	41	.14	36
Patient 2	75	.14	74
Mean	58	.14	55
Therapist D:			
Patient 1	44	.12	32
Patient 2	51	.17	37
Mean	48	.14	35
All therapists:	91	.27	64

n = 64 sessions

expectations rather than of the expectations or activities of particular patients.

It seems to us that this congruence between therapists' expectations and certain quantitative aspects of their actual behavior during the first eight sessions of treatment may enable us to bridge the gap between the attitudinal and the behavioral aspects of the psychotherapy situation. It provides a sort of operational hold upon a particularly elusive problem and it provides a first-order approximation in quantitative terms as to what a therapist means when he says that he is an active or passive therapist. Thus we have found a direct relationship in psychotherapy between an expectational system and an action system.

EFFECTS OF DISSIMILARITIES IN THERAPIST AND PATIENT EXPECTATIONS

We shall now assess the hypothesis that dissimilarity between therapist and patient expectations in given areas disequilibrates the therapeutic system, and that mechanisms are consequently set in motion which are aimed at relieving the strain and restoring equilibrium. We consider socialization of the patient by the therapist to be one of these basic restorative mechanisms.

Therapist communications aimed at patient socialization deal with the process and goals of therapy, i.e., with the rights and obligations of therapist and patient vis-a-vis each other, and with the mechanisms and routines of this special social situation. They are communications concerned with "teaching" the patient the new system of reciprocal role relationships, which we hypothesized as essential to the restoration of system functioning whenever dissimilarities of expectation have created system strain.

We will now present data regarding the effect upon therapist performance of dissimilarities in one dimension of therapist-patient conceptions—that of "activeness."

An index of dissimilarity in conceptions of activeness was constructed, based on five parts of a question asked both of therapist and patient at the beginning of therapy.[1] The value of the index ranges from 0–10, with 0 indicating complete similarity and 10 the highest possible dissimilarity.

Table 23 shows the effect of dissimilarities in therapist-patient "activeness" expectations upon the occurrence of therapist primary system (socializing) communications during the first three hours of therapy.

We observe in Table 23 that our hypothesis is strongly documented. Comparing the two patients for each therapist, we find that whenever there is more dissimilarity with respect to activeness expectations, there is a greater number of therapist primary

TABLE 23

DISSIMILARITIES BETWEEN THERAPIST-PATIENT EXPECTATIONS WITH REGARD TO THERAPIST ACTIVENESS AND THERAPIST PRIMARY SYSTEM REFERENCES

Therapist	*Patient*	*Index of Dissimilarity (ranging from 0–10, with high = dissimilar)*	*Proportion of therapist Primary System References during first three hours of therapy*
A	1	0	.09
	2	2	.27
B	1	1	.16
	2	3	.49
C	1	2	.05
	2	3	.20
D	1	3	.15
	2	4	.19

n = 24 sessions

system references. Furthermore, as might be expected the amount of primary system reference generated by expectational dissimilarity is related to the level of activeness of each therapist. For instance when the index of dissimilarity reaches 3 for one of the active therapists (B), the proportion of his primary system references rises to .49. But for one of the less active therapists (C) when the index of dissimilarity reaches 3, his proportion of primary system references rises to only .20. We conceive the emergence of "role" information to be a direct consequence of dissymmetry in expectations. For purposes of dealing with this problem, we regard dissymmetry of expectation as one kind of disequilibrium and communication centered around the primary system as one form of attempted re-equilibration.

Table 23 reflects the effect of *actual* dissimilarities in expectation. However, we also have data on *anticipated* dissimilarities, gathered to find out whether therapists' communicational acts are affected more by the state of the interaction system than by intra-personality system variables. In other words, will a therapist be more likely to give primary system information when the state of the system requires it (dissimilarity in actual state of expectations) or when he thinks it may be required (anticipated dissimilarity)? The extent to which the therapist anticipates that the patient's view is similar or dissimilar to his own is assessed by two questions consisting of five parts each, asked of the therapist at the beginning of therapy. The therapist is asked: "Consider the following list of activities—will you engage in them often, sometimes, or never in the course of therapy with this particular patient." He is then asked: "From what you know, does the patient think you will engage in these activities often, sometimes, or never?" On the basis of the therapist's answer, an index is constructed which reflects the extent of dissimilarity in expectations anticipated by the therapist. An index value of 0 indicates that the therapist anticipates that the patient's views are wholly like his own, while 10 indicates that he anticipates that they are wholly dissimilar.[2]

Table 24 shows to what extent the anticipation of dissimilarities bears upon the communication process between therapist and patient.

We observe that, except for therapist B, there is no relationship between anticipated dissymmetry and therapist primary references. Further, that the therapist allocates a good portion of his verbal output to the induction of the patient into the primary system even where he does not anticipate dissymmetry.

Comparing Tables 23 and 24 we note that the actual disequilibrium present in the system (dissimilarity of expectation) is highly associated with the extent to which the therapist emphasizes role discussion, but that anticipated disequilibrium on the part of the therapist does not show such a correlation.

TABLE 24
THERAPIST ANTICIPATED DISSIMILARITIES IN EXPECTATION OF ACTIVENESS AND THERAPIST PRIMARY SYSTEM REFERENCES

Therapist	*Patient*	*Index of therapist anticipated dissimilarity (ranging from 0–10, high = dissimilar)*	*Proportion of Primary System References during the first three hours of therapy*
A	1	0	.09
	2	0	.27
B	1	1	.16
	2	4	.49
C	1	4	.05
	2	3	.20
D	1	2	.15
	2	1	.19

n = 24 sessions

The therapist thus aligns his behavior with reference to the actual state of the system of expectations rather than with reference to an anticipated state.

We have shown previously that therapist expectations are reflected in communications, yet we now find that a discrepancy between his own expectations and those he attributes to the patient does not give rise to a change in his pattern of action. We suggest that this is due to the following interactive process. Patient role expectations reflect themselves in patient behavior (communications). Patient expectations that are dissimilar to those of the therapist tend to produce verbalizations indicating strain and disequilibrium. The therapist responds to these communications in such a way as to relieve the strain which they indicate, even though he may not have consciously re-evaluated his own estimate of the patient's expectations.

It then appears that requirements of the action system (as found in the actual situation) take precedence in therapy over intra-psychic factors. We have thus identified another set of latent processes which operate to restore complementarity in the therapeutic interaction. In this case, we have been able to uncover evidence of the "latency" of the process. Although the therapist consciously misjudges the state of the system, he nonetheless behaves in the proper way from the point of view of system maintenance.

NOTES

1. The index was constructed as follows: The therapist is asked "Consider the following list of activities—will you engage in them often, sometimes, or never, in the course of therapy with this particular patient?" The patient is asked "Please indicate for each of the activities described below whether you think the therapist will engage in the activity often, sometimes, or never, during your therapy. The activities include: suggest what to talk about next; prohibit you from doing things he considers inadvisable; counsel or advise you in the management of day-to-day living; explain what therapy is all about." *Scoring:* The answers "often," "sometimes," and "never," are respectively given the numerical values of 3, 2, and 1. The arithmetical differences for any given item between therapist conception and patient conception are then added. The greater the value of the sum of the differences, the higher the dissimilarity in therapist-patient conception of therapist "activeness."

2. The scoring is as follows: The answers "often," "sometimes," and "never" are respectively given the numerical values of 3, 2, and 1. The arithematical differences between therapist expectations and therapist estimate of patient expectations are then added, irrespective of sign. The greater the value of the sum of the differences, the higher the index of therapist anticipated dissimilarity in expectations of activeness.

CHAPTER X

Satisfactory and Unsatisfactory Communication

Proceeding with our analysis of the interrelationships between expectations and communication, we attempted to discriminate between the communication that occurred in sessions that patients rated as more satisfactory and those that patients rated as less satisfactory. The satisfaction that a participant derives from communication is closely related to his expectations (in the sense of wishes). If the communication fulfills these expectations, he will experience some degree of satisfaction. If the communication does not fulfill his expectations in some way and he is thereby disappointed, he will experience dissatisfaction. That is why we would expect patients to rate communication which fulfills expectations as more satisfactory than communications which disappoint them in some way.

Satisfaction with communication is related not only to the occurrence of specific content but also to the process of communicating. Strain in communication results not only from lack of consensus on subject matter, but also from disequilibria in the patterning and flow of communication itself (e.g., from asymmetry in pace of interaction, in continuity of interaction, in verbal output level).

In this chapter, we shall report on the relationship between patient ratings of ease of communication during psychotherapy sessions and some of the actual characteristics of the verbal interchanges in those sessions. The following questions are dealt with:

(1) Does the pattern of verbal communication in psychotherapy sessions rated by patients as proceeding "more easily" differ in character from sessions they rate as proceeding "the same" or "less easily"?

(2) If so, how do they differ with respect to quantity of verbal output, rate of interaction, informational specificity, affective emphasis, and propositional form?

After each of three sessions approximately six weeks apart, each patient was asked to rate the session as follows:

> In comparison with the last two weeks, how did communication between you and the therapist proceed during the hour? About the same? Less easily? More easily?

The findings presented here are based upon an analysis of 23 such panel sessions. The sample thus consists of three sessions for each of eight patients with one session omitted because it was not fully recorded. Patients rated 10 sessions as proceeding "more easily," nine as "about the same," and four as proceeding "less easily." Table 25 summarizes 10 variables differentiating the sessions rated as proceeding "more easily" from those rated as proceeding "the same" or "less easily." It should be borne in mind that the ratings of satisfaction obtained from our patients are comparative or relative ratings rather than absolute ratings of patient satisfaction.[1]

PATTERN OF VERBAL COMMUNICATION

Volume of Verbal Output. On the average, the therapists' verbal output during the therapy sessions rated by patients as proceeding "more easily" was about twice as large as in the sessions rated as proceeding "about the same" or "less easily"

TABLE 25
DIFFERENCES IN COMMUNICATIONAL STRUCTURE AMONG SESSIONS

Description of variable	*For sessions rated as proceeding "more easily"*	*For sessions rated as proceeding "the same" or "less easily"*
1. Average number of therapist propositions per session	90	46 [a]
2. Average number of patient propositions per session	305	242 [b]
3. Average ratio of therapist to patient propositions	.29	.19
4. Average number of exchanges per session	52	34
5. Proportion of therapist propositions that are questions	.30	.37 [a]
6. Proportion of therapist propositions that are highly specific	.37	.23 [a]
7. Proportion of statements in which patient changes the subject	.20	.28 [a]
8. Proportion of therapist propositions that are affective	.40	.21 [a]
9. Proportion of patient propositions that are affective	.27	.23
10. Ratio of therapist to patient affective propositions	.41	.18

n = 23 sessions

All the differences reported hold for each therapist considered separately, except for the case of one therapist with reference to one variable (items 8 and 9). This internal consistency in the findings is perhaps a more valid test of significance than the formal tests presented below.

[a] Difference significant at .01 level (Student's "t" distribution, 2 tail test)

[b] Difference significant at .05 level (Student's "t" distribution, 2 tail test)

(Table 25, item 1), while the verbal output of patients was about 25 percent higher (item 2). The average number of interactions per session was about 50 percent greater in the sessions rated "more easily" (item 4). The ratio of therapist propositions to patient propositions increased on the average from .19 to .29 (item 3). Evidently therapeutic communication is rated by patients as proceeding more easily when the therapist's verbal participation reaches a certain level as measured by verbal output and interaction rate. Also, the more symmetrical (perhaps within optimal ratio limits) the quantitative distribution of verbal participation between the patient and the therapist, the greater the satisfaction the patient experiences with the communication process. Increased participation in treatment is not uniquely determined by the specific nature of the content of the communications exchanged, but also appears to be a function of certain formal characteristics of the communication process itself.

Use of Propositions in the Interrogatory Form. In general, the proportion of therapist propositions in the form of questions was 23 percent higher for sessions in which communication was rated by patients as proceeding "the same" or "less easily" (item 5). The proportion of patient propositions that are questions was low for all sessions (around .04) and there does not appear to be any difference between sessions.

The work of Bales [2] on small problem-solving groups seems relevant here. Bales reported that the proportion of questions occurring in problem-solving sessions with which group members afterwards expressed dissatisfaction was higher than in the sessions with which group members were satisfied.

Since questions are devices by which communication processes are initiated and are also an extremely effective way of turning the initiative over to the other participant, questions increase during treatment when it is necessary to initiate or maintain the communication process, or to turn the initiative over to the other. The burden of responsibility for such activities ordinarily falls upon the therapist. This is especially true when a patient is having difficulty talking and strain has appeared in the communication process. Not only is the increase in the number of questions asked by therapists related to strain or dissatisfaction on the part of the patient, but also, the use of questions helps to eliminate expectational dysymmetry and to restore equilibrium. Of course, it is also possible that an increase in therapist questions may be uncomfortable for the patient and thus increase his dissatisfaction.

Propositional Specificity. Item 6 shows that a greater number of highly specific therapist propositions occur in the sessions rated by patients as having more satisfactory communication.[3]

Two highly limiting categories of propositions, and hence categories regarded as having a high degree of specific informational stimulus value were therapist propositions that excluded specific topics or propositions from further discussion (e.g., "Let's not go into that right now"; "We don't need any other dreams") and propositions in which the therapist provided information or gave interpretation that were not intended to elicit any response.

On the average, the proportion of therapist propositions having such high specific informational stimulus value was 60 percent greater for the sessions in which the communication was rated as having proceeded more easily. Thus patients express more satisfaction with therapeutic sessions in which the therapist's verbal activity is highly structured. High structure or specificity in the therapist's communications is related to patient satisfaction presumably because it provides cognitive clarity for the patient. Precision in informational verbal signals reduces the amount of discontinuity in the communication process. Reduced ambiguity in the therapist's propositions reflects itself in a reduction of anxiety, confusion, and disorientation in the patient's verbal communications. This of course is not necessarily therapeutically desirable.

Continuity of Frame of Reference. Propositions were classified according to systems of reference: the self, the treatment, the family, the past, the present, etc. For example, "Isn't a therapist able to tell me a thing like this?" is a proposition that has the treatment process as its frame of reference. A proposition like "My father yelled at me today" has the family as its frame of reference. Eight categories were used to identify systems of reference. Through identification of the reference system of a proposition, it became possible to ascertain its relevance or congruence to preceding or subsequent propositions. Consistency of system category indicates that discussion of the same subject matter is being continued, and change in system category indicates a change in subject matter.

Item 7, Table 25 shows the frequency with which patients initiate a change of system reference from that of the therapist's preceding statement. Item 7 shows almost a 50 percent greater frequency with which patients initiate changes in system reference in hours rated as the "same" or "less easily."

Consistency of system references in sequences of propositions is an indication of continuity of subject matter. On the other hand, frequent shifts in subject matter—viewed from an interactional standpoint—suggest dissatisfaction and lack of consensus on the part of the patient and the therapist as to what to talk about (psychodynamically, such subject matter shifts may represent patient "resistance," etc.). In the hours during which communication proceeded "more easily," there appears to be an increase in consensus as to what to talk about. This hypothesis is consistent with the idea that informational specificity reduces confusion and misunderstanding, since in the hours rated "more easily," the rise in informational specificity is accompanied by a fall in the frequency of system shifts.

Use of Affective Propositions. As we have noted from time to time, verbal communications concerning affect are regarded as a basic feature of psychotherapeutic interaction, and therapists frequently seek to get their patients to verbalize about feelings. Therapists very rarely discuss their own feelings. Hence, when therapist propositions refer to affect, they take a somewhat different form from those of patients. Therapist affective propositions are oriented to patient feelings. For example: "Tell me why you are crying," "You felt sad," "Resented whom?", etc. Patient affective propositions, on the other hand, refer to their own feelings.

On the average, the proportion of therapist propositions referring to affect was almost 100 percent greater in sessions rated "more easily" than in those rated "the same" or "less easily" (item 8); the average proportion of patient affective propositions was 17 percent greater (item 9).

It will be remembered that therapists A and B were considerably more active verbally with their patients than were therapists C and D. Their mean verbal output, relative verbal output, and mean interaction rates were more than twice as high as those of the two less active therapists. While the proportion of patient affective propositions in sessions rated "more easily" more than doubled (relative to the proportion in sessions rated "the same" or "less easily"), for the four patients of the two active therapists, the proportion of affective statements actually diminished for the two patients of therapist D, one of the less verbally active therapists.

Item 10 shows the ratio of therapist affective propositions to patient affective propositions. The mean ratio is .41 therapist affective propositions for the sessions rated "more easily" and .18 for the sessions rated "the same" or "less easily." A higher ratio of therapist affective propositions indicates that the therapist is verbalizing his concern, recognition, and sensitivity to the patient's feelings. The ratio reflects the proportion of times a therapist initiates or responds to a patient's verbal expression of feelings. Patient satisfaction in therapy is related to the ratio of therapist affective propositions to patient affective propositions. This ratio reflects communicational symmetry and congruence between patient and therapist.

We shall now offer some general hypotheses about why the sessions with the characteristics enumerated above were rated as more satisfactory. These hypotheses relate to two questions:

how disappointment was diminished, and how satisfaction was increased.

1. The pattern of communication in the more satisfying sessions is more nearly similar to that of ordinary social relationships, and so is more in line with the patient's previous experience.

2. In the previous professional interactions in which the patients have participated, the professional participant probably has assumed a role more active and reciprocal than that of a therapist. Therapist behavior thus deviates from what the patient expects of a professional man rendering service.

3. The transference manifestations of therapy prompt the patient to expect the therapist to "give" to the patient. Verbal ouput on the part of the therapist is thus interpreted as a "gift" from the therapist. Therapist passivity and lack of participation is equated with rejection and reacted to with frustration.

4. The patient's substantive problem is that of disorientation with respect to the therapeutic system as well as with respect to the major role systems in which he participates outside of therapy. Therapist feedback in the form of verbalization, interaction, and informationally specific interventions counters this disorientation and increases a sense of satisfaction.

5. Increase in order and continuity in the flow of communication contributes to a sense of achievement and satisfaction.

6. Increase in affective concern on the part of the therapist gives the patient a sense of being understood. Abreaction and catharsis of feelings contribute to the patient's feeling of satisfaction.

NOTES

1. We did not consider it feasible to request the patients to attempt to rate their satisfaction with a session from an absolute point of view because in complying with such a request the patient

would in any case have to rely upon some set of criteria, and we would not know what these were. We also strongly suspect that the patients actually gave us more or less a rating of satisfaction. The consistency of the differences in the communicational patterns found among the therapists between sessions rated as "more easily" and those rated as "the same" or "less easily" is further evidence to support this contention.

2. Parsons, Bales, and Shils, *Working Papers in the Theory of Action,* p. 116.

3. For the purpose of this analysis, Category (6), "Therapist introduces a sequence of new propositions," and Category (8), "Therapist excludes a specific topic," were used as representative of high specificity propositions.

Part Six

CONCLUSION

CHAPTER XI

Some Last Thoughts

Over and above a presentation of data and findings, we consider our research to be in the nature of a demonstration. One of our intentions was to show that the approach and concepts of one discipline (sociology) could contribute to an understanding of problems faced by another discipline (psychiatry).

It seemed to us that the emphasis in the social sciences upon the study of latent system processes, and upon viewing relationships from a vantage point other than that of the participants, could be especially valuable for a deepened understanding of the therapeutic interaction.

This approach to the study of behavior is concisely summarized by Spiegel (a social scientist as well as a psychiatrist) when he says: ". . . much of what occurs in the way of behavior is not under the control of any individual or even set of individuals, but is rather the upshot of complicated processes beyond the ken of anyone involved . . ." The study of such processes is one of the main concerns of social scientists.

Without recapitulating the specific findings of our study, we would like to point out some of the general areas in which the assumption of the social science viewpoint provided insight into the therapeutic relationship.

First we saw that despite major differences in the outlook and the behavior of each therapist and each patient, there are major similarities among therapist-patient pairs in terms of the way the interaction unfolds longitudinally. This finding raises many questions for those who tend to stress differences between therapists in their theoretical orientation and who overemphasize the importance of the "school" to which a therapist belongs as the determinant for what transpires during therapy. It could be claimed that specific acts (techniques) occurring in one kind of therapy and not in another are the significant factors in the "cure" of the patient. From this point of view, it is the "differences" in therapy which count. However, we are inclined to disagree that this is wholly true. If emotional illness is the result of long and continued faulty interaction from childhood on between the patient and a wide variety of his role partners, then it is hard to see how one or another circumscribed aspect of therapist behavior could provide the necessary restorative experience. We believe that the most important contribution of therapy lies in the experience, in the total and recurrent pattern of patient and therapist interaction, extending over an enduring period. The enormous amount of similarity in therapeutic systems suggests to us that what is shared by different therapist-patient pairs may be at least as therapeutic as that which is unique.

Although we have studied only a few variables, and these mostly of a formal kind, they may in turn be correlated with some whose "therapeutic" relevance is more immediately apparent. Thus, the traditional psychiatric variables (e.g., defense, resistance, transference, repression) can be reintroduced in the context of our system-oriented, quantitative approach.

Secondly, we have found a good deal of evidence that therapist and patient interact in the true sense of the term, and that feedback plays an essential role in treatment. Interdependence was demonstrated for many of the variables studied. Those who view therapy as a one way street—with the therapist as witness, observer, and transference object—will have to reexamine their position in the light of these findings. The movement of verbal behavior toward similarity despite the basically asymmetrical definition of therapist-patient role relationships focuses attention on the problem of values. The flow of positive and negative sanctions in therapy—the patterning of reinforcement and extinction of types of verbal responses—needs more empirical study. The exceedingly important part played in therapy by value communications and influence processes needs to be explored further.

A third point clearly follows from the second. Within limits, the requirements of the system take precedence over expectations and conceptions of therapeutic roles. Much of this occurs outside the awareness of the therapist. Often, the realization that he is departing from a preconceived therapeutic position in the interest of maintaining the system follows upon, rather than precedes, the "system-sensitive" act. We believe that this question of system sensitivity versus theory orientation has profound implications for the training of therapists. Some individuals may be better equipped to respond to the requirements of the here-and-now rather than to the requirements of the past. Attention to system responsiveness could very well become a more self-conscious part of therapeutic training. A system-sensitive therapist adjusts his pattern of activities to the activities of the patient and to the demands of the therapy system itself. Ultimately, the therapist establishes that proportion, that ratio, and that mean or equilibrium, with respect to this, that, and the other system variable, which will maintain the therapeutic system within the limits of variation that the system itself necessitates.

What is latent for the personality system are "unconscious processes," while what is latent for the social system are "system processes." By making the patient conscious of these hitherto unconscious personality processes, the therapist increases the patient's adaptive control and flexibility. Our identification of system processes can serve a very similar function for the therapist. By enlarging the therapist's awareness of the processes taking place in the therapeutic systems in which he participates, we may make possible an increased measure of responsiveness and control on his part. In this sense there is no contradiction, as Bales has so insightfully remarked, between the traditional emphasis upon the importance of intra-psychic factors and our attention to social system processes. Each serves equally to broaden our understanding of the process of psychotherapy.

Fourthly, when we applied the deutero-learning hypothesis to the process of psychotherapy, we became aware of psychotherapy as a prototypic role learning situation. It is a situation in which the patient learns the "learning of roles." In this respect too our viewpoint is complementary to that advanced by analytic theorists. Just as analysts consider therapy most fruitful when the patient engages in an easy weaving back and forth between the analytic situation, the current reality situation, and the childhood situation (see Menninger), so do we suggest that therapy achieves its "role learning goals" *to the extent* that the patient is able to transfer what he has learned about role patterns in therapy to other significant role relationships. We do not suggest that the patient need become aware of this level and function of the therapeutic process, but it may be important for therapists to interest themselves in the level of abstractness or concreteness with which role patterns are learned and generalized by their patients. From this point of view it may be detrimental for the patient to become overimpressed with the distinctiveness of the therapeutic situation and fail to recognize its similarity and generic relevance to other role relationships. A patient who learns the patient role too well and on too concrete a level has become oversocialized.

The methodological emphasis of our research is a fifth point that bears mention. We believe that an objective dissection of the therapeutic process is at least in some aspects feasible. Perhaps researchers in the field of psychotherapy have been somewhat overcautious in their concern for the more subtle factors and nuances of the psychotherapy interaction.

It seems to us in the light of our findings that there are many significant gross or molar variables in the psychotherapy situation that lend themselves to quantitative management. The quantitatively more conspicuous structures and their effects need to be defined and explored further before more refined efforts are undertaken. While these elements do not comprise the totality of the therapeutic situation, they do offer a sort of overall frame of reference or structure providing a perspective from which to examine the details as they are filled in.

Although our sample was not large enough to provide sufficient data to establish "norms" for therapeutic behavior, it does suggest a sort of rough first order approximation in quantitative terms of some of the communicational parameters of the psychotherapy situation. For example, we now have some idea of how active a therapist is, who regards himself as active, and what a therapist means when he says that he is passive. The analysis of a larger and more diverse sample of therapeutic hours from different therapists would provide us with criteria data against which a given therapist or a given therapy could be measured. Moreover, some inter-therapist differences which were not explored in the present work could be pinned down more precisely. It might even eventually become possible to characterize and describe different therapeutic styles and different therapeutic techniques in terms of an empirically established pattern of quantities.

In the course of the research we have, of course, had second thoughts about what additional work needed to be done within the limits of this kind of research. We mention three of these prospects here.

We recorded only the early part of therapy, the first eight months. Intensive study of the second and third year of therapy in terms of the dimensions outlined would also be rewarding.

In addition to characterizing the units as propositions, statements, and sessions, we would have liked to score sequences of propositions and elements. Such sequence scoring would have helped us to pinpoint changes in the patient word mirror. Does he, at point T_2, convey thoughts and feelings in configurations that differ from the configurations evident at T_1?

The idea that deutero-learning is one of the latent functions of therapy became fully clear to us only later in our research. This important idea needs more empirical documentation in the verbatim transcripts than we have been able to give.

Data of a quantitative sort are particularly suited to an analysis of psychotherapy in terms of learning theory. Reinforcement, extinction, and other conditioning phenomena can be operationally applied to the therapy situation and numerous learning-theory hypotheses can be thereby tested. For example, the distinction between nondirective and directive psychotherapy may possibly be related to operant and respondent types of learning; these in turn might be defined in terms of who initiates subject changes or in terms of some of the interaction process categories (e.g., patient asks, therapist gives; or vice versa).

We have throughout the book stressed the great complexity of interaction processes involving even as few as two persons. In terms of number, size, and possibility of variation in interrelationships, we have drawn an analogy with the human organism. We know that many disciplines are involved in the study of the organism, and that many of the insights which have emerged have often been due to collaboration among these disciplines. However, the proper mode of collaboration with respect to many problems has yet to be achieved. The study of social interaction, in any given context, can similarly profit from such cross-disciplinary attention, though some problems may still resist collaborative efforts.

The productiveness of this approach has already been demonstrated on a variety of fronts. The anthropologist, Gregory Bateson, is bringing tools for the identification of patterns, forms, and rules of behavior from his own discipline to the study of families with schizophrenic members. He has shown that, using proper tools, much that was considered "senseless" in the behavior of schizophrenic patients with their families and with others can be demonstrated to be meaningful forms of conduct, in terms of the kind of interaction experiences which these patients have had.

Birdwhistell, another anthropologist, has begun to codify behaviors ranging from voice quality to body movement. The work of Nathan Ackerman in New York and John Spiegel in Boston, who are attempting to assemble concepts from a variety of disciplines into a new vocabulary describing family interaction and family therapy, represents another cross-disciplinary attack on this problem.

We are not for a moment overlooking the importance of the conceptual tools already available to those charged with specific tasks within their own disciplines. Important contributions have been made and will continue to be made by psychoanalytic psychiatry and psychotherapy, with their emphasis upon freeing patients from damaging inhibitions, irrational fears, and rigid defenses; their commitment to the uncovering of unconscious motives and the lifting of repressions; and their objective of making the patient more capable of mature functioning in work and love. Their contribution is without question a significant one. All we are saying is that it cannot provide a complete picture of the structure of behavior in the therapeutic relationship, let alone in other interpersonal relationships, and that it should not lay claim to doing so. Drawing attention to the contribution that another discipline can make to these tasks is the latent content of this book.

Bibliography

Ashby, W. Ross, *Design for a Brain* (New York, John Wiley and Sons, 1954).

Bales, Robert F., "In Conference," *Harvard Business Review*, XXXII (March–April, 1954), 44–51.

Bales, Robert F., *Interaction Process Analysis: A Method for Study of Small Groups* (Cambridge, Mass., Addison Wesley Press, 1950).

Bales, Robert F., letter to Conrad Arensberg, mimeographed copy made available by Robert F. Bales (1950).

Bales, Robert F., and Fred L. Strodtbeck, "Phases in Group Problem Solving," *Journal of Abnormal and Social Psychology*, XLVI (September, 1951), 311–322.

Bales, Robert F., and Phillip E. Slater, "Role Differentiation in Small Groups," *Family: Socialization and Interaction Process* ed. by Talcott Parsons and Robert F. Bales (Glencoe, Ill., The Free Press, 1955).

Bales, Robert F., *The Strategy of Small Group Research*, mimeographed (undated).

Bateson, Gregory, "Social Planning and the Concept of 'Deutero-Learning,'" *Conference on Science, Philosophy, and Religion*, Second Symposium (1942).

Bernstein, Arnold, "On the Nature of Psychotherapy," *Doubleday Papers in Psychology* (New York, Doubleday, 1954).

Bertalanffy, Ludwig von, "Some Biological Considerations on the Problem of Mental Illness," *Bulletin of the Menninger Clinic*, Vol. XXIII, No. 2 (March, 1959).

Bertalanffy, Ludwig von, "General System Theory," *Life, Language, Law*, ed. by Richard W. Taylor (Yellow Springs, Ohio, The Antioch Press, 1957).

Bordin, Edward S., "Ambiguity as a Therapeutic Variable," *Journal of Consulting Psychology*, LXX (1955), 9–15.

Brosin, Henry W., "Information Theory and Clinical Medicine,"

Current Trends in Information Theory (Pittsburgh, University of Pittsburgh Press, 1953).

Butterfield, Herbert, *The Origins of Modern Science* (London, Bell, 1949).

Cannon, Walter B., *The Wisdom of the Body* (New York, W. W. Norton, 1932).

Chapple, Elliot D., with Conrad M. Arensberg, "Measuring Human Relations: An Introduction to the Study of the Interaction of Individuals," *Genetic Psychology Monograph,* XXII (1940), 3–147.

Davis, Fred, "Definitions of Time and Recovery in Paralytic Polio Convalescence," *American Journal of Sociology,* Vol. LXI, No. 6 (May, 1956), 582–587.

Davis, Kingsley, *Human Society* (New York, The Macmillan Company, 1950).

Deutsch, Felix, *Applied Psychoanalysis* (New York, Grune and Stratton, 1947).

Dollard, John, and O. Hobart Mowrer, "A Method of Measuring Tension in Written Documents," *Journal of Abnormal Psychology,* XLII (1947), 3–32.

Emerson, Alfred E., "Homeostasis and Comparison of Systems," *Toward a Unified Theory of Human Behavior,* ed. by Roy R. Grinker (New York, Basic Books, 1956).

Freud, Sigmund, "Further Recommendations on the Technique of Psychoanalysis (1913)," *Collected Papers of Sigmund Freud,* Vol. II (London, Hogarth Press, 1949).

Greenspoon, Joel, "The Reinforcing Effect of Two Spoken Sounds on the Frequency of Two Responses," *American Journal of Psychology,* LXVIII (1956), 409–416.

Grinker, Roy R., ed., *Toward a Unified Theory of Human Behavior* (New York, Basic Books, 1956).

Homans, George C., *The Human Group* (New York, Harcourt Brace, 1950).

Katz, Daniel, and Herbert Hyman, "Industrial Morale and Public Opinion Methods," *International Journal of Opinion and Attitude Research,* Vol. I, No. 3, 13–30.

Lennard, Henry L., "Concepts of Interaction: An Examination of Interrelationships," unpublished Ph.D. dissertation, Columbia University (1955).

Lennard, Henry L., "Studies in Factual Interviewing," Vol. V (ed. by

Lee Wiggins and Kurt Back), submitted to Human Resources Research Institute, USAF (1953).

Lennard, Henry L., Murray E. Jarvik, and Harold A. Abramson, "Lysergic Acid Diethylamide (LSD-25): XII. A Preliminary Statement of its Effects upon Interpersonal Communication," *Journal of Psychology*, XLI (1956), 185–198.

McCarthy, Mary, "Ghostly Father I Confess," *The Company She Keeps* (Dell).

Menninger, Karl, *Theory of Psychoanalytic Technique* (New York, Basic Books, 1958).

Merton, Robert K., "The Role Set: Problems in Sociological Theory," *The British Journal of Sociology*, Vol. VIII, No. 2 (June, 1957), pp. 106–120.

Merton, Robert K., George G. Reader, and Patricia L. Kendall, editors, *The Student Physician* (Cambridge, Mass., Harvard University Press, 1957).

Miller, George, "Psycholinguistics," *Handbook of Social Psychology*, ed. by Gardner Lindzey (Cambridge, Mass., Addison Wesley, 1954).

Murray, Edward J., "A Content-Analysis Method for Study Psychotherapy," *Psychological Monographs*, Vol. LXX, No. 13 (1956).

Nagel, Ernest, "A Formalization of Functionalism," *Logic Without Metaphysics* (Glencoe, Illinois, The Free Press, 1956), 247–283.

Newcomb, Theodore M., "An Approach to the Study of Communicative Acts," *Psychological Review*, LX (1953), 393–404.

Parsons, Talcott, *The Social System* (Glencoe, Illinois, The Free Press, 1951).

Parsons, Talcott, Robert F. Bales, and Edward A. Shils, editors, *Working Papers in the Theory of Action* (Glencoe, Illinois, The Free Press, 1953).

Parsons, Talcott, and Edward A. Shils, editors, *Toward a General Theory of Action* (Cambridge, Mass., Harvard University Press, 1952).

Reid, John R., "The Problem of Values in Psychoanalysis," *The American Journal of Psychoanalysis*, XV, No. 2 (1955).

Rogers, Carl R., *Counseling and Psychotherapy* (Boston, Houghton Mifflin, 1942).

Roth, Julius A., "The Time Table of the T.B. Patient," unpublished manuscript.

Ruesch, Jurgen, *Disturbed Communication* (New York, W. W. Norton, 1957).

Salzinger, Kurt, and Pisoni, S., "Reinforcement of Affect Responses of Schizophrenics During the Clinical Interview," paper read at the 1957 annual meeting of the Eastern Psychological Association.

Spiegel, John P., "Interpersonal Influences within the Family," *Group Processes, Transactions of the Third Conference,* ed. by Bertram Schaffner, M.D. (New York, Josiah Macy, Jr., Foundation, 1957).

Spiegel, John P., "The Social Roles of Doctor and Patient in Psychoanalysis and Psychotherapy," *Psychiatry,* XVII (1954), 369–376.

Spiegel, John P., "The Resolution of Role Conflict within the Family," *The Patient and the Mental Hospital,* ed. by M. Greenblatt, D. J. Levinson, and R. H. Williams (Glencoe, Illinois, The Free Press, 1957).

Sullivan, Harry Stack, *Conceptions of Modern Psychiatry* (Washington, D.C., William A. White Psychiatric Foundation, 1947).

Sullivan, Harry Stack, *The Psychiatric Interview* (New York, W. W. Norton, 1954).

Wolberg, Lewis R., *The Technique of Psychotherapy* (New York, Grune and Stratton, 1954).

Zeigarnik, B., "Über das Behalten von Erledigten und Unerledigten Handlungen. K. Lewin Untersuchungen zur Handlungs und Affektpsychologie, III," *Psychologische Forschungen,* IX (1927), 1–86.

Zelditch, Morris, "A Note on the Analysis of Equilibrium Systems," *Family: Socialization and Interaction Process* (Glencoe, Illinois, The Free Press, 1955), 401–408.

Zetterberg, Hans L., "An Action Theory," unpublished manuscript, Columbia University (1955).

Index